Entire Sanctification:
The Distinctive Doctrine of Wesleyanism

ENTIRE SANCTIFICATION:

The Distinctive Doctrine of Wesleyanism

by

J. Kenneth Grider, Ph.D.

Beacon Hill Press of Kansas City
Kansas City, Missouri

1980

Permission to quote from the following copyrighted versions of the Bible is acknowledged with appreciation:

The Holy Bible, New International Version (NIV), copyright © 1978 by the New York International Bible Society.

The New English Bible (NEB), © The Delegates of the Oxford University Press and The Syndics of the Cambridge University Press, 1961, 1970.

The New American Standard Bible (NASB), © The Lockman Foundation, 1960, 1962, 1968, 1971, 1972, 1973, 1975. Unless otherwise indicated, all scripture quotations in this volume are from this version.

The Revised Standard Version of the Bible (RSV), copyright 1946, 1952, © 1971, 1973.

10   9   8   7   6   5   4

Contents

Dedication

To Ken, our son

Foreword

One would be hard pressed to name a person better qualified to deal with the subject matter of this book. Professor Grider brings to his task more than three decades of involvement with the subject of holiness both professionally and personally. Not only has he chosen his subject carefully, but he has also focused on entire sanctification as the most definitive aspect of the subject. Consequently his treatment bypasses the more generally accepted facets in order to deal adequately with disputed areas.

He is surely right in selecting "entire sanctification" as the most crucial and definitive nomenclature within the parameters of scriptural holiness. His treatment is to be commended for both its affirmation and its denials: breaking with tradition when the evidence so leads and reaffirming it in areas where needed.

Especially valuable is his use of "baptism language" in elucidating the subject of sanctification, since recent studies have debated this issue at some length. Here he differs from John Wesley and contemporary charismatic movements, yet makes a convincing case for his position.

Of great practical value is the chapter dealing with contemporary misunderstandings. In his rejection of the identification of the Pauline "old man" with original sin, he is on solid exegetical ground. (If the "new man" refers to Paul's "new creature" surely the "old man" implies the unregenerate). Helpful also is his clarification of Paul's condition before he became "in Christ."

Not surprisingly, Dr. Grider writes more from a theological than an exegetical perspective (despite his competence with Greek). He appears to be interacting with issues raised within the Holiness movement rather than appealing to evangelical

Christians in general. Admittedly he writes with "a certain Nazarene interest and flavor," but at the same time his insights have a relevance far outside his own denomination.

Author and publisher are to be commended for making these mature and judicious insights available to the general public.

—George Allen Turner

Preface

In this book, my attempt has been to write a theology of entire sanctification, Wesleyanism's most distinctive doctrine.

I have not given formal treatments of the philosophy or the psychology of the doctrine, feeling that some of the turns theology has taken in these times make those interests much less important than they were considered to be a generation ago.

I have not treated any doctrines except that of entire sanctification. By this I mean I have not developed the holiness of God, or the doctrine of sin, or any other doctrine, just because it is germane to entire sanctification. Those and other doctrines do get worked into the study, but only in the course of treating actual aspects of the doctrine of entire sanctification.

I have devoted two chapters to the relationship between the baptism with the Holy Spirit and entire sanctification. This emphasis is in part because the Pentecostals and the Neo-Pentecostals also emphasize the Spirit baptism, though their understanding of what is effected by that baptism differs from our holiness view. My emphasis is also in part because the long-held holiness view that entire sanctification is wrought by the baptism with the Holy Spirit, is a subject of considerable discussion in holiness circles these days.

The Holiness movement has been different from John Wesley, particularly in identifying entire sanctification with a personal baptism of or with the Holy Spirit. I feel that in amending Mr. Wesley at this point, the holiness writers have been scriptural. I feel also that in doing this they have been following a Wesley tradition or style. Since he himself changed certain aspects of his entire sanctification teaching as he went along, adding numerous notations in later years which indicate how his understanding had changed, it might be more un-Wesleyan than Wesleyan to "swallow him whole."

While other holiness books have in part occasioned this one, it is hoped that this one might occasion still further holiness theologizing.

I have kept in mind the entire Holiness movement, as I have written the book. The reader will find, however, a certain Nazarene interest and flavor which may be excusable because I am an elder-teacher of the Church of the Nazarene. The *New American Standard Bible* is quoted throughout this volume, unless it is otherwise noted.

I express gratitude to Professor William Miller, Nazarene Theological Seminary librarian, who helped me obtain materials; to my student assistant, Mr. Floyd Cunningham, who also made resources available to me; and to my students, Mr. Westley Bichsel and Mr. Philip Patalano, for the indexes. Virginia, my wife of 37 years, contributed much by encouraging me, by her interest, by seeing to it that I was free to do the work, and by reading the manuscript as my dictionary and my first critic on content and style. Dr. Fred Parker, long the book editor of the Nazarene Publishing House, helped immensely in a reduction of the manuscript's length and in making it more readable.

—J. Kenneth Grider

Chapter 1

An Introduction:
The Distinctive Doctrine

Entire sanctification is essentially defined as an instantaneous cleansing from Adamic sin, and an empowerment, which Christian believers may receive, by faith, through the baptism with the Holy Spirit.[1]

The apostle Paul was surely referring to this experience when he said to the believers at Thessalonica, "Now may the God of peace Himself sanctify you entirely; and may your spirit and soul and body be preserved complete, without blame at the coming of our Lord Jesus Christ. Faithful is He who calls you, and He also will bring it to pass" (1 Thess. 5:23-24).

A. More than a Theological Provincialism

This teaching and experience is more than what Boston University's A. C. Knudson called it: a "theological provincialism" of Methodism. It is the teaching which peculiarly completes Martin Luther's 16th-century attempt to reform Christian doctrine according to its New Testament pattern. While it belonged to the man from Wittenberg to reestablish the doctrine of justification by faith, it belonged to the man from Epworth, Mr. Wesley, to reestablish the doctrine that, once justified by faith, believers may be sanctified wholly by faith—instantaneously, and in this life.

---

1. While this doctrine is associated with the teachings of Methodism's founder, John Wesley (1703-91), he himself did not teach that it is effected by the baptism with the Holy Spirit. This will be discussed later.

B. *Wesley's Distinctive Contribution*

This doctrine is John Wesley's most distinctive contribution to the Christian faith. But Wesley is distinctive in several other ways as well. For one thing, he implemented Arminianism evangelistically and popularized it. James Arminius (c. 1560-1609) died at about age 50, after only six years in a professorship, and before seeing the evangelistic implications of his doctrine that *anyone* may be saved, not just the ones God previously elected. In Wesley, the man who rode horses all over England and beyond (affectionately saying about one of them that it would probably live on in heaven), we have "Arminianism on fire."[2] Indeed, it is so much "on fire" that it was not altogether improper for university students in England to be asked to write on the subject, "Since Wesley, we are all Arminians."[3] In response to the question, "What do the Arminians hold?" someone responded with the quip, "All the best bishoprics and deaneries of England."[4] Said in jest, it nevertheless underscored the success of Arminianism largely attributable to the leadership of Wesley.

Significantly, Wesley named the periodical he started late in his life, The *Arminian Magazine*. Through its pages—and otherwise—he popularized the teachings of "the quiet Dutchman" whose views had been earlier even outlawed for a brief time in Holland. This was a distinctive contribution, especially in view of the fact that, in America, Methodism's emphasis on human freedom appealed to the frontier mind. Small wonder that it spread westward and grew so phenomenally.

Other distinctives are associated with that five-feet-five Oxford don with the warmed heart and austere but winsome ways. Doctrinally, this certainly included his special emphasis upon the witness of the Spirit. Organizationally, it included the class meetings, predecessors to the popular small-group meetings of our day.

Yet the doctrine of entire sanctification, Christian perfection, perfect love—whichever handle is put onto it—is John Wesley's most distinctive contribution to the Christian faith. From a

---

2. Gerald O. McCulloh, ed., *Man's Faith and Freedom: The Theological Influence of Jacobus Arminius* (New York: Abingdon Press, 1962), p. 61.

3. *Ibid.*, p. 46.

4. *Ibid.*, p. 47.

theological standpoint, Wesley must be mentioned among such great figures of the Christian faith as Augustine, Luther, and Calvin. Wesley wrote a sustained treatment of original sin, which is basic to the doctrine of entire sanctification, since that is what is "expelled," as Wesley liked to say, at that time. He spent much time putting together his teachings on entire sanctification in his *A Plain Account of Christian Perfection*. He also treated the subject in sermons, often discussed it in letters, and otherwise contributed to its emphasis in the Societies. Also, he wrote, translated, and emended hymns, and encouraged the writing and the singing of his brother Charles's holiness hymns—most of which expressed yearning for this grace.

C. *Methodism's Distinctive Emphasis*

While Methodism today sometimes treats the doctrine of entire sanctification as something out of the past not altogether welcome in its creed, it has not always been this way. Early, when Methodism was turning a secularized England right side up, and when it was helping the American frontier to put its best foot forward, the doctrine was importantly Methodism's raison d'etre.

John Wesley himself, of course, called it the "grand depositum which God has lodged with the people called Methodists." Philip Schaff spoke of it as Methodism's "last and crowning doctrine."[5] Nolan B. Harmon says it has been "the one specific doctrinal contribution which Methodism has made to the Church universal. . . . In all else we have been . . . glad and energetic followers. . . . But in this one doctrine we stand by ourselves and utter a teaching that reaches up fearlessly and touches the very Scepter of God."[6] Harald Lindstrom, whose *Wesley and Sanctification* is one of the most significant books on entire sanctification, says that while Wesley is "primarily concerned with justification and sanctification as the two fundamental doctrines, . . . it is undoubtedly sanctification that receives major attention."[7] Even the quite liberal Francis J.

---

5. Quoted in John L. Peters, *Christian Perfection and American Methodism* (New York: Abingdon Press, 1956), p. 196.

6. *Ibid.*

7. *Ibid.*, pp. 8-9.

McConnell felt that the doctrine as an ideal constitutes "the glory of Methodism."[8]

D. *Motivation of the Holiness Movement*

Without question, it is the doctrine and experience of entire sanctification that has been the chief motivation of the Holiness movement in America, beginning a little before the middle of the 19th century. It was not the only message, however. Antislavery views motivated many, such as Luther Lee and others who broke off from Methodism a few years after its 1836 decision to permit slaveholding. The liberation of women was also a special interest of America's Holiness movement. Among the earliest women admitted as students to college were those welcomed at Oberlin College in Ohio. One of these, Antonette Brown, who in 1853 was ordained to the ministry, was perhaps the first woman ever formally ordained.[9]

Temperance, then abstinence, then prohibition, also became a special interest of the "holiness people." Frances Willard was herself a part of this movement. This anti-alcohol issue was often a big plank in the platform of the teachers and preachers and writers who ministered under the auspices of the National Camp Meeting Association and the National Holiness Association.

Yet people in the Holiness movement held as their fondest aim to "spread scriptural holiness" over the land. They seemed sometimes to think of "spreading" it the way you spread butter on a slice of bread. But they were using, of course, an expression of Mr. Wesley himself. And when you think of Methodism's earlier circuit riders, who were often unmarried because it sometimes took several months to cover their circuit of preaching points, it was indeed a bit like "spreading" holiness doctrine. If it had to be spread thin, they still spread it. And it tasted good to people as the nation advanced westward and dug in.

Active in the promulgation of holiness teachings in the early days of the movement was Phoebe Palmer, who wrote and spoke much, and edited *Guide to Holiness.* Charles G. Finney and Asa Mahan, of Oberlin College, helped immensely

---

8. *Ibid.,* p. 9.
9. See Donald Dayton, *Discovering an Evangelical Heritage* (New York: Harper & Row, 1976), p. 88.

to popularize these teachings. This movement's emphasis, like that of Wesley, was that entire sanctification is attainable "now and by simple faith."[10]

E. *Wesleyanism's New Breed*

The Holiness movement today needs to guard against a too-easy conscience on social issues, such as legalized abortion. It needs to guard against a tendency to depreciate the significance of the sacraments. It needs to guard against a neglect of the economically deprived in the inner cities. And it needs to guard against seeking social status.

Yet the doctrine and experience of entire sanctification, Wesleyanism's peculiar genius, is being propagated these days by a savory new breed of church folk. Fewer eccentrics are in leadership, and fewer autocrats. Fewer biblically unsupportable ideas are circulated.

Only a generation or so ago, philosophy and psychology were sometimes presented as brothers of just about equal status with Scripture in the arsenal of supports offered for the doctrine and experience of entire sanctification. Today the really respected supports, and rightly so, are biblical ones—with, of course, a healthy respect for the opinion of authorities in the doctrine's history.

Holiness publications of recent vintage are often more scholarly. Especially is this so of several of the Ph.D. dissertations on holiness that have been published.[11]

A better-educated holiness ministry also obtains—persons likely to be college or seminary graduates, some of whom are entering into Doctor of Ministry programs, with many others in continuing education courses.

The Wesleyan Theological Society has for nearly 15 years fostered academic conversation among the Holiness movement's scholars, with some 1,100 persons in its membership.

---

10. See Peters, *Christian Perfection and American Methodism,* p. 189.

11. These include the following: Harald Lindstrom, *Wesley and Sanctification* (London: The Epworth Press, 1946); George A. Turner, *The More Excellent Way* (Winona Lake, Ind.: Light and Life Press, 1952); John L. Peters, *Christian Perfection and American Methodism;* Leo G. Cox, *John Wesley's Concept of Perfection* (Kansas City: Beacon Hill Press of Kansas City, 1964); Charles E. Jones, *Perfectionist Persuasion: The Holiness Movement and American Methodism* (Metuchen, N.J.: The Scarecrow Press, 1974).

It issues a theological journal and encourages scholarly publications. And it is a subsidiary of the Christian Holiness Association (formerly the National Holiness Association), which itself fosters seminars and publications in its promotion of scriptural holiness.

These and other developments would indicate unabated, and indeed revitalized interest in the doctrine of entire sanctification. Importantly, there is an openness to new and enriching concepts related to it while still maintaining its historic foundations.

Chapter 2

Components of the Experience

Even as one's work, or one's life, or one's marriage, say, can be viewed from a number of angles, so the doctrine and experience of entire sanctification can be viewed from several perspectives. In this chapter, the doctrine will be studied from a variety of these viewpoints.

A. *A Separation to God's Use*

The Hebrew root *KDSH,* for "holiness," occurs some 830 times in the Old Testament—which is exceedingly frequent. The word seems to mean to "cut off," "separate," perhaps "elevate." Actually, it has not been possible for scholars to ascertain what the word's etymological history is. Yet George A. Turner suggests—and most scholars no doubt would agree. with him—that its etymology is "not essential to understanding its actual Old Testament usage."[1]

Perhaps this word for "holiness," which basically seems to mean "separation," "originally had no ethical associations."[2] One indication of this is in the fact that prostitutes, who were connected with pagan temples as a way of serving the god or

---

1. Turner, *More Excellent Way,* p. 22.
2. See *ibid.,* where Turner quotes Rudolph Otto, *The Idea of the Holy,* 1908, pp. 6, 25. A. C. Knudson, in his *The Religious Teaching of the Old Testament* (New York: Abingdon Press, 1918), gives considerable support for this understanding, although he and many others do need to be studied by evangelicals with the realization that they work according to the Documentary Hypothesis view.

gods of fertility, were called "holy ones."[3] They were not themselves holy, in an ethical sense, as the biblical mind would understand the matter. But they were called "holy" because they were persons separated to a special use for the so-called gods.

In Israel's own usage, some would argue that there was from very early times an ethical content in *KDSH* when applied to persons—and that the ethical requirement for such persons is implied by the blemishless requirement in animals to be used as sacrifices (see 2 Chron. 29:5, 15-19; also Lev. 22:21-25; Deut. 15:21; Mal. 1:8).

Regarding the quite apparent basic meaning of the word as "separation," Turner says, "In every one of the more than eight hundred places where this sort of root is used in the Old Testament the meaning of separation is permissible; in many instances it is demanded."[4]

The counterpart New Testament verb for "holiness," *hagiadzo,* "to make holy," includes in its meaning "to separate," while it very frequently also means to cleanse or to purify from a moral standpoint.

Several uses of the term, with its cognates, indicate the idea of separation to God's use. That is quite evidently the meaning in John 17:19 where Jesus says, "For their sakes I sanctify Myself." We are often told that Jesus was without sin (e.g., 2 Cor. 5:21). He was perfect—a spotless Lamb who was to make the sacrifice of himself for us—so He needed no sanctification in the sense of purification from sin. As human, though—as *fully* human—He did need to sanctify himself in the sense of setting himself apart to be used of God the Father and going to the Cross for us.

A similar use of a cognate of the word appears in the Lord's Prayer. We say, "Hallowed be Thy name" (Matt. 6:9). In that prayer we are telling God that we want Him (one who is himself bound up with His name) to be set apart from and above everything else that touches our lives. As E. F. Walker puts it, "When Peter enjoins to 'sanctify Christ as Lord in your hearts' (1 Pet. 3:15), the meaning is that we are to give the Lord Jesus

---

3. See 2 Kings 23:7.
4. Turner, *More Excellent Way,* p. 22.

the supreme place in the throne of our being—'that all may honor the Son, even as they honor the Father' (John 5:23)."[5]

It is well known that the same word is used where Jesus prays for the disciples, "Sanctify them in ["through," KJV] the truth" (John 17:17). This was no doubt a prayer for their cleansing from original sin, a cleansing that was to occur on Pentecost Day. Numerous things within this prayer for them, and earlier said about them, show that they had already been sanctified in the sense of initial sanctification (since they were converted) and in the sense of their being set apart for God's use. They had been called out of the world and had been ordained for ministry already. Christge would not have needed to pray for their sanctification in that sense.   *Separate*

A cognate of "sanctify" as meaning separation to the Father's use is also quite evidently what we have in John 10:36. *from* ?
There, the Father has "sanctified" Jesus. Jesus was about to *for* ?
be stoned by "the Jews," for what they called blasphemy, since *because* ?
they said He was setting himself up as God. Jesus asks, "Do you say of Him, whom the Father sanctified and sent into the world, 'You are blaspheming'; because I said, 'I am the Son of God'?"

Similar usage is found in 1 Cor. 7:14: "The unbelieving husband is sanctified through his wife, and the unbelieving wife is sanctified through her believing husband; or otherwise your children are unclean, but now they are holy." Here, in the sense of separation to God's use, marriage is made holy by the faithfulness of the believing partner.

---

5. Edward F. Walker, *Sanctify Them,* revised by J. Kenneth Grider (Beacon Hill Press of Kansas City, 1968), pp. 20-21. In this book, in this connection, we also read: "The Bible uses *sanctify* in the sense of *hallowing, honoring, glorifying,* but such is not the meaning in the passage under study in this little book (John 17:17). In Isaiah 5:16 we read: 'But the Lord of hosts shall be exalted in judgment, and God that is holy shall be sanctified in righteousness.' Of course this cannot mean that the holy God is made holy, but that He is to be recognized as holy. . . . So in Isa. 29:23: 'They shall sanctify my name, and sanctify the Holy One of Jacob, and shall fear the God of Israel.' This refers to the reverencing of His holy name. We read in Ezek. 36:23, 'And I will sanctify my great name . . . when . . . I shall be sanctified in you.' Here we are to understand that, when the Lord is hallowed among His own people as He should be, He will make His holy name to be revered where formerly it had been profaned" (p. 20).

B. A Cleansing from Original Sin

Several views flourish, on how God's grace deals with original sin.

1. *Suppressionism.* This position, held by the majority of Reformed evangelicals, is that original sin remains in the believer, but that God helps him more and more to suppress its outworkings. Their interpretation of the apostle Paul, in Rom. 7:14 ff., is that he is talking about indwelling sin in himself (vv. 17, 20), and describing his present experience.

2. *Counteractionism.* This is the so-called Keswick theory. As in suppressionism, this view holds that original sin is not dealt with radically, but that, when the Scriptures speak of its being cleansed, or whatever, the meaning is that it remains as a condition in the believer. However, the Keswick view is that the Holy Spirit, who also indwells him, counteracts the original sin so that it is not expressed as it would be otherwise.

This teaching has been associated with the conventions held at Keswick, England, from about 1875 onwards. In the very early years of America's Holiness movement, Asa Mahan was an exponent of this view. Though professing to be Wesleyan, he was exceedingly weak on the matter of any radical treatment for original sin in the baptism of the Holy Spirit. It should be said, however, that the Keswickian position is probably closer to that of Wesleyanism than has often been granted.[6]

3. *Oberlin Theology.* Oberlin College, in Ohio, was for some decades the chief center of gravity of America's Holiness movement. The two principal figures at Oberlin were Charles G. Finney and Asa Mahan.

As a person educated to be a lawyer, Finney seemed to think he was teaching entire sanctification in its authentic form, but it was not precisely so. Although he sometimes taught moral inability apart from grace, he did not always teach the doctrine of original sin, a racial fall in Adam, as it has been taught classically in all the main branches of Christianity. He

---

6. Richard Taylor, who would not be expected to depart very far from holiness orthodoxy, wrote a paper for an area National Holiness Association seminar in the early 1960s, in which he supported through research a view that the Keswick and the Wesleyan views are exceedingly similar.

sometimes tended to be Pelagian and humanistic, as for example, when he wrote, "The human will is free, therefore men have power or ability to do all their duty."[7] Yet if, because of original sin, we are enslaved to Satan prior to conversion, prevenient grace is necessary if we are to perform our known duties.[8] On this matter, the Nazarene Articles of Faith read much as do other historic Christian confessions: "We believe that . . . through the fall of Adam he [man] became depraved so that he cannot now turn and prepare himself by his own natural strength . . . But we also believe that the grace of God through Jesus Christ is freely bestowed upon all men, enabling all who will to turn from sin to righteousness" (Article V).

Asa Mahan is different from Finney in one special regard. He elaborates much more meticulously the teaching of Scripture that it is the baptism of the Holy Spirit which effects entire sanctification. Finney had done this somewhat, in articles in the *Oberlin Evangelist,* but in his later and more thorough treatment of entire sanctification (in his *Systematic Theology*) he is usually content to ply the reader with logic rather than with Scripture. Mahan, on the other hand, works carefully with Scripture teaching, in his major work of 1870, *The Baptism of the Holy Ghost.*[9]

Yet Mahan was exceedingly weak on a cleansing from original sin in entire sanctification. His emphasis was that our "Pentecost" yields an enduement of power. The fact is that in Mahan's book, *Christian Perfection,* written 30 years earlier, before he had begun to associate the Spirit baptism with Christian perfection, there is more on entire sanctification as cleansing than in his later writing.

4. *Radical Cleansing from Original Sin.* Though John Wesley did not identify entire sanctification with a "baptism with the Holy Spirit," he was clear on the matter that God cleanses us from original sin radically. He spoke of "love filling

---

7. Charles G. Finney, *Lectures on Systematic Theology* (Oberlin, Ohio: E. J. Goodrich, 1887, abridged reprint of the second edition of 1851), p. 325.

8. A. M. Hills, one of Finney's students, was justified in his understanding that Finney was usually a "volitionalist" to such extent that he humanistically expected man to be able to do whatever he wanted to do. See his *Life of Charles G. Finney* (Cincinnati: Revivalist Office, 1902), p. 224.

9. See Asa Mahan, *The Baptism of the Holy Ghost* (New York: George Hughes and Co., 1870).

the heart, expelling [not just suppressing] pride, anger, desire, self-will."[10] Wesley also wrote much about the body of sin being destroyed.

J. A. Wood, in both the 1861 and 1880 editions of his now classic *Perfect Love,* taught clearly the radical cleansing from Adamic sin through entire sanctification. It was only in the later edition of his great work that he viewed entire sanctification as being wrought by the Spirit baptism. Yet in both editions he is an "eradicationist." In the revised (1880) edition he writes:

> In the grace of justification, sins, as acts of transgression, are *pardoned.* In the grace of sanctification, sin, as a malady, is *removed,* so that the heart is pure. In the nature of the case, the eradication of sin in principle from the human heart completes the Christian character. When guilt is forgiven in justification, and all pollution is removed in entire sanctification, so that grace possesses the heart and nothing contrary to grace, then the moral condition is reached to which the Scriptures give the name of perfection, or entire sanctification.[11]

Original sin is "destroyed," for Wood, using Paul's expression. "It [entire sanctification] is a state of sweet rest from all conflict between the will and the conscience. 'The body of sin has been destroyed,' and the soul has peace with itself—inward quietude."[12]

Wood often uses "eradicate" and "exterminate" and "extirpate" as expressions of how God's grace radically deals with original sin.

J. B. Chapman, author of several books on entire sanctification, teaches a radical view concerning the removal of original sin.

> We hold that sin as a condition or state is like a virus in the blood, and is not in any way essential to one's life, is not inseparably bound up with life, and is, in fact, a menace to life and a hindrance to the functioning of life in both the body and the spirit. This virus can therefore be removed, the blood stream can be purged, and the person can still live; in fact, can live more abundantly in both

---

10. John Wesley, *A Plain Account of Christian Perfection* (Chicago: The Christian Witness Co.), p. 84.

11. J. A. Wood, *Perfect Love* (Chicago: Christian Witness Co., 1880), p. 34.

12. *Ibid.,* p. 128.

body and spirit than before. This doctrine of sin lays foundation for a doctrine of sanctification that is both consistent and practical.[13]

The witness of many later theologians could be added, such as George Allen Turner, J. Glenn Gould, W. T. Purkiser, S. S. White, and Richard S. Taylor, all of whom have clearly taught that one component of the second work of grace is a real and radical cleansing from original sin.[14]

At conversion, one's own acts of sin are forgiven; but at that time, for various reasons, original sin (Adamic, racial sin) is not cleansed, not even in part, according to Scripture. It is our own sins that are our concern when we are repenting and asking the gracious God to forgive us. At that time, we are rebels, and are laying down our arms.

However, to be cleansed from original sin through the baptism with the Holy Spirit, we approach God not as rebels who need to be forgiven, but as children of His who need to be cleansed. As children of God, we consecrate ourselves to His use and, by faith (even as for justification), we receive cleansing from this Adamic sin.

John the Baptist said:

> As for me, I baptize you in water for repentance, but He who is coming after me is mightier than I, and I am not *even* fit to remove His sandals; He Himself will baptize you with the Holy Spirit and fire. And His winnowing fork is in His hand, and He will thoroughly clean His threshing floor; and He will gather His wheat into the barn, but He will burn up the chaff with unquenchable fire (Matt 3: 11-12).

Much is here which suggests that, when this baptism would occur, the believing disciples would receive a deep-down, thorough cleansing. The "fire" of v. 11 is symbolic of such a cleansing. It might denote a deeper, more radical cleansing than water does (which of course also symbolizes cleansing). There is exegetical support for this. The passage itself further

MORE than WATER

---

13. J. B. Chapman, *The Terminology of Holiness* (Kansas City: Beacon Hill Press, 1947), p. 27.

14. See Turner, *More Excellent Way*, p. 195; J. Glenn Gould, *The Whole Counsel of God* (Kansas City: Beacon Hill Press, 1945), p. 56; W. T. Purkiser, *Sanctification and its Synonyms: Studies in the Biblical Theology of Holiness* (Kansas City: Beacon Hill Press, 1961), p. 43. He here quotes from a chapel address by Taylor at Pasadena College, fall, 1956; S. S. White, *Eradication Defined, Explained, Authenticated* (Kansas City: Beacon Hill Press, 1954).

refers to cleansing in v. 12 where we read that when this baptism will occur, Christ will have a "winnowing fork . . . in His hand," and "He will thoroughly clean His threshing floor," and "burn up the chaff" (v. 12).

Matthew 3:11-12 is corollary to John 7:37-39, where we read:

> Now on the last day, the great *day* of the feast, Jesus stood and cried out, saying, "If any man is thirsty, let him come to Me and drink. He who believes in Me, as the Scripture said, 'From his innermost being shall flow rivers of living water.' But this He spoke of the Spirit, whom those who believed on Him were to receive [at Pentecost]; for the Spirit was not yet *given,* because Jesus was not yet glorified."

This also speaks of cleansing—a cleansing of the "thirsty" who are to "drink" the proper water, so that from their "innermost being," the heart (Mark 7:21-23), "rivers of living water" will flow forth. And we are told that Jesus was speaking of "the Spirit" who had not been given in Pentecostal fullness, since Christ had not yet gone to the Father.

Acts 15:8-9 is another significant scripture passage which connects cleansing, or purification, with the Pentecostal baptism with the Holy Spirit. Peter explains: "God, who knows the heart, bore witness to them, giving them the Holy Spirit, just as He also did to us; and He made no distinction between us [at Pentecost] and them [at Cornelius's house, Acts 10], cleansing their hearts by faith." As Pentecost is summed up, in this reference, the sundry languages and the blowing winds are passed by and the significant point made that their hearts were "cleansed."

C. The Baptism with the Holy Spirit

Spirit baptism is a most significant component of entire sanctification doctrine. It is this baptism with the Holy Spirit that occasions, or effects, entire sanctification. While some holiness people say that the two are equated, the two should perhaps, more accurately, be considered simultaneous.

The baptism with the Holy Spirit is indeed one of the six names given for entire sanctification in the Nazarene Articles of Faith. Yet that does not mean that the two are the same. Entire sanctification is called the baptism with the Holy Spirit in part because this baptism occasions it, and in part because this baptism is so significant an aspect of what happens when a believer receives entire sanctification. At that time, among the other things that happen, a believer is dipped into, immersed into, has poured out upon him, the Holy Spirit. In effect, this means that the Holy Spirit then indwells the believer pervasively. In that same instant, original sin is cleansed away. Indeed, it is this very baptism with fire that cleanses (Matt. 3: 11-12; Acts 2:1-4; 15:8-9), or that brings about the cleansing away of the perverse, recalcitrant, estranging state of original sin—for the indwelling sin (Rom. 7:17, 20) must be expelled in order for the Holy Spirit to indwell the believer in such fullness.

This Spirit baptism fulfills what Joel had prophesied about (2:28)—and Jeremiah (c. 31), Ezekiel (c. 36), John the Baptist (Matt. 3:11-12), and Jesus (John 14:17; Acts 1:4-5). It is the fulfillment of the prayer of Jesus for His disciples: "Sanctify them" (John 17:17). It is probably also the fulfillment of the post-Resurrection prayerful statement of Jesus to His disciples: "Receive the Holy Spirit" (John 20:22).[15]

D. *An Empowerment*

In the Holiness movement our greatest emphasis has been on the cleansing from original sin which results from the baptism with the Holy Spirit. This has been a proper emphasis. It is because of this cleansing through the baptism with the Holy Spirit that this experience is called entire sanctification.

But we have also known that power, as well as purity, is associated with the baptism with the Holy Spirit. Acts 1:8 makes this clear to us, where we read, "You will receive power when the Holy Spirit has come upon you; and you shall be My witnesses both in Jerusalem, and in all Judea and Samaria, and even to the remotest part of the earth."

With respect to this passage, Beverly Carradine makes this unique observation:

> There are two works accomplished in the Baptism of the Holy Ghost as received by the Christian believer—

---

15. Some Wesleyans do not feel that anyone could have been given the first work of grace prior to Christ's death and resurrection, but at the same time they believe that Pentecost was a second work of grace. So they take the position that Christ's "receive the Holy Spirit" was the time of the conversion of the apostles.

"purifying the heart" and "enduement of power." In Christ's case, there was no inbred sin or moral taint of any kind to be purged away. All that could take place with His spotless human nature was the empowering of the Spirit. Hence the Holy Ghost did not descend on Him with fire, as in the case of the disciples, but as a dove. That the Savior did receive the enduement of power then, is seen by the clear statements of Scripture. It was after this memorable morning that it is said that "He went forth in the *power* of the Spirit."[16]

But we have not strongly emphasized the power. Even the Calvinists, who do not believe in purification or cleansing from original sin as associated with our "Pentecost," have emphasized the power given the Spirit-baptized believers. Some of them, such as Charles E. Fuller, have said that this baptism happens at one's conversion. Others, such as Harold John Ockenga, have taught that the baptism with the Spirit is subsequent to conversion. In either case, their emphasis is upon one's empowerment—especially for witnessing for Christ.

The Holiness movement could well emphasize this aspect of one's "Pentecost" more than it does. And it could well admit that the power means power for witnessing for Christ. It is more than just the power to live a holy life. No doubt this latter thought has some truth in it, but it implies that we might not be expected to live a holy, separated-to-God life after our initial conversion experience. Also, this viewpoint has given us a soft sell on witnessing for Christ. But Acts 1:8 states clearly that the power is for witnessing: "You shall receive power when the Holy Spirit has come upon you and you shall be My witnesses."

While some people are of milder temperament than others, and more introvertish by nature, a power for witnessing is given us, along with purity, when we as believers receive our personal Pentecost.

Jesus Christ sits on the edge of the lips of all of us, waiting to be gossiped about. He will give us the power to tell people, in more or less winsome ways, whose we are, and to help us as we seek to lead them to Christ.

---

16. See Beverly Carradine, *The Second Blessing in Symbol* (Louisville, Ky.: Picket Publishing Co., 1896), pp. 17-18.

E. A Sealing

Entire sanctification is also described in Scripture as a sealing—somewhat in 1 Cor. 1:21-22 and Eph. 4:30, but clearly in Eph. 1:13.

In the first of these, Paul seems to refer to two aspects of this second work of grace—establishment and sealing—and connects them both with the giving of the Holy Spirit. Paul writes, "He who establishes us with you in Christ and anointed us is God, who also sealed us and gave us the Spirit in our hearts as a pledge" (2 Cor. 1:21-22).

While Paul refers to sealing in Eph. 4:30, he does so with more explicitness in Eph. 1:13, where we read: "In Him, you also, after listening to the message of truth, the gospel of your salvation—having also believed, you were sealed in Him with the Holy Spirit of promise."

Although Calvinists often interpret this and the other references to sealing as suggesting eternal security, holiness theologians consider the figure to be a reference to one aspect of entire sanctification. It is to be noted that some of these Christians being addressed, had listened to the "gospel" of "salvation"; had "also believed"; and after that, had been "sealed in Him with the Holy Spirit of promise." This is a reference to the Holy Spirit who had been promised by Joel (2:28), by Ezekiel (c. 36), by John the Baptist (Matt. 3:11-12), and by Jesus (Acts 1:4-5).

Sealing as a symbol suggests ownership—that the believer is then truly owned by God, as a sealed letter is owned by its addressee. Sealing also suggests approval. Thus a school's seal is placed upon a person's diploma. Once a believer is completely yielded to God (Rom. 12:1-2), he is truly owned by God (see Gal. 5:24); and once the carnal mind, original sin, is expelled, a believer is approved of God in a deeper sense than obtains when his acts of sin are forgiven at his justification.

F. A Growing State of Right Relationship

The relational theologians rightly hold that original sin and its counterpart, holiness, are relational matters. Original sin is a propensity or bias or inclination toward acts of sin, due to an estrangement from God. It exists because certain ministries of the Holy Spirit have been withdrawn due to Adam's sin. Being deprived of those ministries, we became positively depraved: "inclined to evil and that continually." And holiness, too, is relational. It is a correcting of original sin's alienation. As relational, this holiness is not a static state with no dynamic for development in it. Nor is it a state in the sense that its continuance is assured from one moment to the next whether or not the person continues his consecration and obedient trust.

Some have suggested that it is misleading to consider original sin and holiness experience as states. They want to avoid the implication that they are substantive in nature—that is, real, phenomenal substances. But to call them states does not at all imply that they are static, or that they are substances that can be weighed or measured.

Concerning original sin, we can use such terms for its cleansing as "eradication" or "extirpation" or "extermination" or "removal" or "destruction," without suggesting that the original sin itself is physical or quantitative in nature.

The old analogy in which forgiveness of acts of sin is like getting the tree cut down and that being cleansed from original sin is like getting the stump pulled out is a proper and graphic analogy of what happens in the two works of grace. It might even be considered scriptural, since the writer of Hebrews tells us to pursue after "the sanctification" and to "see to it that . . . no root of bitterness springing up causes trouble" (13:14-15). When Jesus said, "From within, out of the heart of men, proceed the evil thoughts, fornications, thefts," etc. (Mark 7:21), He was probably saying that the deep-seated racial sin issues in sins that can be seen.

If we cannot use physical analogies to illustrate spiritual truths we are somewhat hamstrung. Were this the case, Jesus would not have been able to use physical birth as analogous to the spiritual birth as He did in teaching Nicodemus (John 3). Paul could not have used a seed's dying in order to come forth as a plant, as analogous to the bodily resurrection, as he did in 1 Cor. 15:33 ff. These are only two of countless such analogies in Scripture.

To call sanctification a "state" does not imply a static condition. The state of matrimony does not prohibit two people in the state of love as well as in the state of marriage from having a living, vital, growing relationship with each other. The state of one's health does not mean that one's metabolism is static. The state of the nation is never a static one.

Regarding Adamic sin as a state, Scripture supports such a view in numerous ways. When Paul speaks of "indwelling sin" (Rom. 7:17, 20) which legislates him, to which he feels himself enslaved, he is implying that it is a state. His use of nouns with reference to it also implies this: for example, "the sin" (all through Romans 6); the carnal mind (Romans 8); carnality (1 Corinthians 3); the "flesh" (Gal. 5:17, 24, etc.); "the law of sin and of death" (Rom. 8:2). Paul even personifies it quite often, as in its deceiving him (Rom. 7:11).

J. A. Wood called perfect love "this state of rest."[17] He further said, "It is only when our all is upon the altar of consecration that we can be in a state of sanctification."[18] He also calls perfect love "this gracious state," and adds, *"Negatively, it is that state which excludes all sin from the heart."*[19]

Statements of numerous other holiness writers could be marshalled to affirm that entire sanctification is a state as well as a relationship, and that it is, by all means, a *growing* state. It is only when the recalcitrant original sin is expelled that Christian growth toward a rich and fruitful maturity can best take place.

G. A Perfection

Another component of entire sanctification is perfection. This experience makes a believer perfect, but, of course, only in a certain sense. It does not make us perfect in the sense that we thereafter have perfect judgment, or perfect ethical conduct. We are perfect in the sense that a metal is perfect when alloys are separated from it so that the metal is all of one kind. When the carnal nature is cleansed away, we are perfect in the sense of having a pure human nature—without the infection of that human nature which carnality occasions. Christians are urged in Scripture to go on to perfection (Heb. 6:1), and to be perfect as our Heavenly Father is (Matt. 5:48).

To be perfect sometimes designates the resurrected state. It seems to be used as a synonym of the *pneumatikoi*, the

---

17. Wood, *Perfect Love*, p. 128.
18. *Ibid.*, p. 227.
19. *Ibid.*, p. 34.

spiritual ones, in distinction from the carnal Christians (1 Cor. 3:1 ff.). Paul seems to have had special meetings with the *hoi teleioi,* the "perfect ones," according to several passages in the Corinthian correspondence (1 Cor. 2:6; 14:23; see also 1 Cor. 14:16; 2:12). These are Christians who have received cleansing from Adamic sin through the full indwelling of the Spirit.

Insofar as words for "perfection" can be translated as maturity, as the RSV does at Phil. 3:15, I agree with H. Orton Wiley that it means maturity, not in the usual sense of ripeness of Christian character, but in the sense of adulthood—the way a young person attains to his maturity or majority or full adulthood at age 21.[20]

It must be mentioned that there are occasions when the New Testament uses perfection to mean perfect conduct, as in Jas. 3:2, where we read: "If any one does not stumble in what he says, he is a perfect man, able to bridle the whole body as well." Yet in the theological parlance of the Holiness movement, that is not the kind of perfection we are talking about. You would not have had whole groups of people perfect in that sense, whom Paul would meet with in special services—the New Testament's counterpart of the Salvation Army holiness meeting. Besides, it is implied, in James, here, that no one is perfect in this sense. We read, "We all stumble in many *ways*. If any one does not stumble in what he says, he is a perfect man" (Jas. 3:2).

Although a few New Testament uses of the term are similar to what we mean in the English when we speak of perfection, the usual New Testament usage as what already characterizes some Christians is what we are talking about in the Holiness movement when we speak of "perfection." It refers to those whose carnal nature has been expelled, so that the nature is not a mixture of the human and the carnal. It refers to those who have received entire sanctification as a second definite work of grace. Thus, for example, Paul includes himself, and at least some to whom he is writing, as among the perfect, in Phil. 3:15 (see also 1 John 4:16-18).

John Wesley himself found that the term "perfection" was badly misunderstood. That is why, in a letter written in 1756, 31 years into his ministry, he said, "I have no particular fond-

---

20. See H. Orton Wiley, *The Epistle to the Hebrews* (Kansas City: Beacon Hill Press, 1959), p. 203.

ness for the term." To say the least, it has not been an altogether helpful term in our holiness tradition.

H. *An Establishing Experience*

Often, entire sanctification has been called "the establishing grace." This is based importantly on 1 Thess. 3:13, where Paul says to believers, "So that He may establish your hearts unblamable in holiness before our God and Father at the coming of our Lord Jesus with all His saints." It is in part based on Rom. 5:1-5, where Paul refers to a grace, received subsequently to justification, in which a person is enabled to "stand"—that is, to stand fast in his faith. This establishment, this being enabled to stand fast, is due to the cleansing away of original sin—which inclines a person to be averse to God.

The Christian who has been sanctified wholly can fall completely from saving grace. But just as surely, such a person is wonderfully enabled *not* to fall from grace.

I. *The Component of Love*

Still another constituent of entire sanctification is love. The second work of grace makes it possible for us to love God with all our heart and mind and soul and strength (see Deut. 30:6; Matt. 22:36-39), and others as ourselves. Wesley emphasized this aspect of entire sanctification experience, often calling the second blessing "perfect love." He appreciated First John very much, quoting from it frequently. Importantly, this was because of its emphasis upon love, and perfect love (1 John 4:8).

J. *The Social Component*

John Wesley knew of no authentic holiness that had no social implications. He himself started a credit union. He practiced medicine in a somewhat more-than-amateurish way, devising even an encyclopedia of health that enjoys some significance in the history of medical literature. He wrote a book on the value of electrical shocks for both mental and physical illnesses. A rule for his Societies was that their members should patronize each other in business. He published Christian literature at low cost with the poor in mind.

His last letter was an encouragement to Wilberforce to

keep up the fight against legalized slavery in England. This letter helped the great abolitionist and might have had a certain significance in England's abolishing slavery in 1806, 15 years after Wesley's death and six decades before it was abolished in America.

George A. Turner even suggests, in what might be a somewhat extreme statement, that "historically, Methodism has been as distinctive for its social service as it has for spreading Scriptural holiness." He says, "Perhaps next to the Quakers, the Methodists can claim credit for the emergence of the 'social conscience.' Thus it was quite natural that Methodism's first child, the Salvation Army, immediately began to dispense 'soup, soap, and salvation,' but they still found time for the weekly 'Holiness Meeting.' "[21]

William Booth, who started the Salvation Army, was first a Methodist. He had been an apprentice "pawn shop" boy and then a fully experienced one, who could not fleece the poor anymore, and became as good a friend as the poor person ever had. He took the gospel of holiness to London's streets and its streetwalkers, and applied the Christian faith in ways that were realistically helpful to needy persons.

Before the middle of the 19th century and somewhat later, according to research by Timothy L. Smith,[22] Donald Dayton,[23] and others, it was persons in the Methodistic-holiness tradition who were in the vanguard of the abolitionist, feminist, and temperance-abstinence movements. At a time when, at Princeton, Hodge and other Calvinists were finding biblical bases for holding slaves, many holiness people were breaking off from Methodism because of her 1836 decision permitting slaveholding. At that time at Oberlin, the holiness giants were going all out to free both the slaves and women.

It is the Holiness movement's consuming interest in implementing the gospel socially that inclined it to preach holiness and millennialism in its postmillennial form—that things are to get better and better. Jonathan Blanchard, long president of Wheaton College, then under the auspices of the Holiness

---

21. Turner, *More Excellent Way,* p. 259.

22. See Timothy L. Smith, *Revivalism and Social Reform in Mid-Nineteenth Century America* (New York: Abingdon Press, 1957).

23. See Donald W. Dayton, *Discovering an Evangelical Heritage* (New York: Harper and Row, 1976).

movement, preached holiness, and preached its social implementation in ways consistent with his postmillennial view. Phineas Bresee, who later started the Church of the Nazarene (1895), was postmillennial, and so optimistic that he would greet a person with a bright "Good morning" even if it was nighttime.

Old-timers of the Holiness movement tell us that at around our century's turn you would hardly feel free to testify at mid-week service if you did not have something to report on the social implementation of the holiness gospel. The holiness people also put many of their "eggs" into the education basket because of their "social" persuasion.

Bresee left Methodism in order to work in a kind of rescue mission. And he soon left that mission to found the Church of the Nazarene—among the familied poor. It was Bresee's social interests that caused him to yearn, most of all, to start holiness work in the great American cities. He was even much more interested in doing this than in fostering world missions.

Evidence abounds that the holiness people have not gone to sleep on social issues. It is true that because Walter Rauschenbusch and other modernists emphasized social-gospel issues, many of the holiness people thought that they themselves should not do so. And many of the holiness people became pre-millennialists, believing that things would get worse and worse before Jesus comes, so they did not want to go all out to help things get better and better.

At present, however, even though the Holiness movement is largely premillennial, it is in a period of renewed zest for social holiness. The newspaper-type magazine, the *Epworth Pulpit,* whose raison d'etre is to encourage the social implementation of Christian faith, is issued under holiness auspices. The Church of the Nazarene, so significant a denomination within the Holiness movement, has made General Assembly declarations on such matters as race relations, abortion, and drug use. Its Christian Action teams are often sent into inner-city areas for summer work—a kind of ministry that has now developed into more than short-term summer projects. The work of Tom Nees in the nation's capital that ministers to D.C.'s unpeople who keep looking up from the bottom of our society is in keeping with this renewed zest. So is Paul Moore's ministry in the Lamb's Club off Times Square in New York City.

Chapter 3

The Nomenclature of Wesleyanism

Wesley's movement itself, and the later outworkings of it in the Holiness movement, has always been plagued by "nomenclaturitus." Its terminology has often been misunderstood. Sometimes its terms and phrases have been misappropriated. The perfectly good term *Pentecostal,* for example, is now generally applied to tongues-speaking people, narrowing its use considerably.

We turn, then, to a discussion of the more common terms used to designate Wesleyanism's distinctive teaching.

1. Perfection or Christian Perfection

The term *perfection,* or, as often added to by Wesley and others, *Christian perfection,* is one of the many names for the doctrine of entire sanctification. Perfection is a biblical word, certainly. We are exhorted to go on to "perfection" (Heb. 6:1). We are to be "perfect" (Matt. 5:48), the way our Heavenly Father is, perhaps by loving our enemies (Matt. 5:44). There is, of course, much other such reference to our being perfect, such as 1 Cor. 2:6; Phil. 3:15; 2 Tim. 3:17; etc.

Aside from a given possible contextual meaning as in Matt. 5:43-48, to be perfect, in the New Testament sense, is to have attained the maturity[1] of Christian adulthood by being cleansed

---

1. Note RSV's translation as "mature," e.g., Phil. 3:15. And note that H. Orton Wiley, in his *The Epistle to the Hebrews,* p. 203, suggests that the *hoi teleioi,* the perfect ones, are mature persons—not in the sense of spiritual richness that comes with growth, but in the sense that at age 21 a person is mature in the sense of attaining to his full adulthood.

of Adamic sin. As a metal is perfect when there is no alloy in it, so we believers are "perfect" when our human nature has had cleansed from it that infection of the human nature known as the carnal nature (see Romans 8; 1 Corinthians 3; Gal. 5:17, 24).

God does not make us perfect in our conduct in the sense that it is faultless. Our conduct is perfect only in the sense that our hearts from which such conduct issues are perfect—not being motivated by the carnal nature. At the same time, the conduct is often much less than correct, or much less spiritually sensitive, than it ought to be. As Mr. Wesley was forced to explain often, this kind of perfection is consistent with "infirmities" of varying kinds. So, he wrote: "I say again, let this Christian perfection appear in its own shape, and who will fight against it?"[2]

Thus, while *perfection* is a term often used in Scripture, it unfortunately suggests to "outsiders" a life that is perfect in the fullest possible sense.

2. Perfect Love

A term similar to "perfection" (and "Christian perfection") is *perfect love*. In Scripture, it is referred to mostly in First John. There we read, "Whoever confesses that Jesus is the Son of God, God abides in him, and he in God" (4:15). This appears to be a reference to the first work of grace—conversion. John then refers to what Wesleyans have come to call entire sanctification when he adds something to this, about being "perfected." He says, "And [in addition to this] we have come to know and have believed the love which God has for us. God is love, and the one who abides in love abides in God, and God abides in him" (1 John 4:16). John continues: "By this, love is perfected with us, that we may have confidence in the day of judgment; because as He is, so also are we in this world" (4:17). Then John calls this special kind of love "perfect love." He writes, "There is no fear in love; but perfect love casts out fear, because fear involves punishment, and the one who fears is not perfected in love" (4:18).

It is passages such as this that caused Wesley to refer to

---

2. Wesley, *Plain Account*, p. 107.

perfect = pure

First John more than to any other New Testament book, in his
A Plain Account of Christian Perfection. Wesleyans in general,
also, have at least found rich entire sanctification teachings in
First John—although not, in general, to the extent that Wesley
did.

However, the phrase "perfect love," although used by the
apostle John, is misleading to many people who suppose that
we mean that our expressions of love to God and others are
absolutely flawless. We only mean, however, that such love is
not mixed with carnal motivations.

3. *The Second Blessing*

Another term is *the second blessing.* It underscores the fact
that entire sanctification is indeed received subsequent to the
time of our conversion. It is a special kind of "blessing." Some
have incorrectly thought that the term finds scriptural support
in 2 Cor. 1:15. J. A. Wood, in the 1880 edition of his book *Perfect Love,* wrote, quoting the KJV:

> The apostle also teaches that "second grace" in 2 Cor.
> 1:15: "And in this confidence 1 was minded to come unto
> you before that you might have a second benefit" (margin,
> "second grace"). The original word, *"Barin"* [he means
> *Charin* from the Greek] here translated "benefit," is trans-
> lated grace one hundred and thirty-one times in the New
> Testament, and is never rendered "benefit", only in this
> single instance, and then is corrected by inserting "grace"
> in the margin.[3]

In the same era of the Holiness movement Beverly Carradine added to this kind of exegesis. He wrote:

> If King James' translator had been truer to the original
> in 2 Corinthians 1:15, we would have today the words "sec-
> ond grace" instead of "second benefit." The Greek word
> translated "benefit" is *charis.* If any Greek scholar should
> be asked what this word meant in the original, he would
> never reply "benefit," but "grace," "divine grace," "divine
> gift," etc.[4]

John Barker, the British Methodist evangelist of recent

---

3. Wood, *Perfect Love,* p. 197.
4. Wood had said 131 times. They are both talking about *charis* in its
various forms.

times, in his *This Is the Will of God,* takes the same kind of view, as have others between Carradine and Barker.[5]

It is correct that the word *charin,* found here, from *charis,* is almost always translated "grace," yet it must be admitted that such a translation here would not fit the context. The context clearly suggests that Paul is talking about a second benefit, or blessing, from his visiting them a second time. The NASB makes the matter clear: "In this confidence I intended at first to come to you, that you might twice receive a blessing; that is, to pass your way into Macedonia, and again from Macedonia to come to you, and by you to be helped on my journey to Judea" (2 Cor. 1:15-16). The NIV makes it even more clear: "Because I was confident of this [of their appreciation of him], I planned to visit you first so that you might benefit twice. I planned to visit you on my way to Macedonia and to come back to you from Macedonia, and then to have you send me on my way [with a good offering] to Judea" (2 Cor. 1:15-16).

Besides its being an evident reference to a second benefit to them from a further visit of the apostle, the next paragraph suggests that, at least largely, the people were already in the grace of entire sanctification. He says, "Now He who establishes us with you in Christ and anointed us is God . . . who also sealed us and gave *us* the Spirit in our hearts as a pledge" (2 Cor. 1:21-22). They had already been "sealed," which is a concomitant of the second work of grace (see Eph. 1:13).

Because some have tried to get holiness "mileage" out of the "second benefit" reference in 2 Cor. 1:15, the term "second blessing" has had about it a certain question. In fact some opponents of second blessing holiness have liked to say that they too have received a second blessing, and a third, and a fourth, and so on. Beverly Carradine's response to such comment was that he too had received many blessings—but that he had received a thousand or so of those blessings before he had received the second blessing.[6]

4. *The Second Work of Grace*

Very similar to the "second blessing" is the designation

5. John Barker, *This Is the Will of God* (London: Epworth Press, 1954), p. 52.

6. See Carradine, *Second Blessing in Symbol,* pp. 17-18.

second work of grace. This is a much more appropriate term, for it has the advantage of being more general. It includes all the concomitants of holiness doctrine, such as the baptism with the Holy Spirit, cleansing from original sin, empowerment, and sealing.

Unfortunately, Pentecostals in general also believe in a second work of grace in which they, as believers, are "baptized in the Holy Spirit" and speak in tongues. In this connection, Frederick Dale Bruner writes, "It appears that majority Pentecostalism absorbed from its Methodist parentage the convictions of the subsequent and instantaneous experience and transferred them bodily from Wesley's sanctification to their baptism in the Holy Spirit. In any case, both Methodism and Pentecostalism put their emphasis theologically someplace after justification."[7] The difference is that Pentecostalism does not include cleansing from original sin but rather tongues-speaking.

5. Christian Holiness

A very appropriate name for the doctrine of entire sanctification is *Christian holiness.* The cover of the *Preacher's Magazine,* for a long time, has used this term in its motto: "Proclaiming Christian Holiness."

One advantage of the term is that it is not offensive to outsiders.[8] Lutherans, Mennonites, Calvinists, Presbyterians, Anglicans—even Roman Catholics—all teach, and even emphasize, Christian holiness of some sort. But, though it does not turn people off, neither does it "turn them on." It is vague and

---

7. Frederick Dale Bruner, *A Theology of the Holy Spirit* (Grand Rapids: Wm. B. Erdmans, 1970), p. 38.

8. A similar inoffensive term—even beguiling—is in Hannah Whitall Smith, *The Christian's Secret of a Happy Life* (Westwood, N.J.: Fleming H. Revell, n.d.). More than 3,000,000 copies of this book have sold, making it by far the most widely used of all holiness books. Indeed, until recent years, it enjoyed one of the widest circulations of any book—second to the *Pilgrim's Progress* and Charles Sheldon's *In His Steps,* but not to many others. Probably the other most widely circulated holiness book is Chester Arthur's *Tongue of Fire,* which was published in at least 12 languages. Neither Hannah Smith's book nor Arthur's, however, are very definitively or specifically or expressly on entire sanctification. That is the chief doctrine which these authors are elucidating in these books. But they do so in disguised ways—this being somewhat more so, in Hannah Smith's classic. You have to search all through, as a reader, to be confident that the Christian's secret of a happy life is to receive sanctification.

broad, with few specifics. It's a ball park the size of the Pacific Ocean.

6. Holiness

The name *holiness* is widely used of Wesleyan Christians, and has been for over a century. The Wesleyans have been known as the "holiness people," and the Wesleyan denominations have been known as holiness churches. That movement which started around 1835, and gathered much momentum in the 1860s and beyond, has been known as the Holiness movement.

But for all that, it is still not precise in meaning. All denominations believe in holiness in some sense, though they would not espouse the doctrine of entire sanctification. Even the Wesleyans often mean something much broader by *holiness* than they do by *entire sanctification.* In popular usage, the two are synonymous; but technically, holiness is begun in the first work of grace (or even in prevenient grace) and it continues, as growth in grace, after entire sanctification.

7. Scriptural Holiness

When entire sanctification is called "scriptural holiness," the meaning is not much sharper. The addition of the adjective "scriptural" helps to underscore the principal source of the doctrine, and advertises that the person is a loyal, "true believer," fully orthodox kind of holiness person.

8. Second Blessing Holiness

Of all the terms with *holiness* in them, this is perhaps the most definitive. It suggests that this grace is received subsequent to the first work of grace. It defines *holiness* in such a way that it could only describe the Wesleyan tradition and no other. It would exclude the Pentecostal teaching, in which, as we have seen, there is also a second work of grace, because Pentecostals do not refer to this work of grace as holiness. It would exclude what Roman Catholics (and others) would mean by *holiness,* since it is called a "second blessing" kind.

This is not what one would consider a scholarly term. It is a "true believer" kind of designation, often used in personal testimony.

9. *Our "Canaan"*

The use of *Canaan,* or the *Canaan Land experience (Beulah* or *Beulah Land* being simply synonyms), as a designation for entire sanctification is a poetic adaptation of an event mentioned often in Scripture (see Hebrews 2—4). According to this symbolism, the deliverance of the Israelites from their Egyptian slavery typifies our deliverance from bondage to sin and Satan at our conversion; and crossing over the Jordan river and entering into the land of Canaan typifies entering into the experience of entire sanctification. The analogies have about them a certain plausibility, too. Being delivered from Egyptian bondage is indeed analogous to being delivered from a cruel taskmaster who is Satan.

After having had a marvelous deliverance from their bondage to Egypt's Pharaoh, Israel was finally led across the Jordan and given a land that "flowed with milk and honey." This was giving something positive to the delivered people, and even so, those delivered from sin's slavery in conversion are indeed given, positively, an inheritance—in entire sanctification. They are enabled to live a holy life.

The problem here is that there is nothing very exegetically compelling about such an interpretation. One must sort of "reach for it" to interpret it this way and so it is not very convincing to someone not yet convinced about two works of grace. Indeed, many interpret Israel's entering into Canaan much differently. Calvinistic evangelicals view Israel's crossing over the Jordan river as a type of physical death. To them, Canaan, or Beulah, where milk and honey flows, is heaven.

10. *Wesleyanism*

As with so many other designations for entire sanctification, to call it *Wesleyanism* has both advantages and disadvantages. The special advantage is to have one's beliefs associated with a person who is almost comparable to Martin Luther in significance. Abraham Lincoln is perhaps best known as believing that the American union should be preserved, so for one of that day to say that he was a "Lincolnite" would be widely understood. He would be associating himself with the well-known philosophy of a popular figure. Something like that is involved when we holiness people call ourselves "Wesleyans."

And a person does not need to agree with his spiritual forebear in all respects in order to associate himself with that figure. Calvinists, for example, might differ with John Calvin on some aspect of the doctrine of absolute sovereignty, and still properly be called Calvinists. So those in the Holiness movement may properly call themselves Wesleyans, even though, on entire sanctification, they would probably not hold identical positions with Wesley, particularly at the point of its relationship to the baptism with the Holy Spirit.

11. *The Baptism with the Holy Spirit*

This term is, by and large, an American addition to John Wesley's teachings. In our using it, we declare our belief that this is the way in which entire sanctification happens. The term is roughly biblical, and within the Holiness movement has long been associated with the doctrine of entire sanctification.

The chief disadvantage in using the term is that the Pentecostals and neo-Pentecostals use only a slightly different phrase, "the baptism *in* the Holy Spirit," to mean something quite different. They do not believe that it cleanses from original sin, but incorrectly teach that one receives at the time either an initial evidence in tongues-speaking, or a special tongues-speaking gift.

12. *Heart Purity*

Though this designation for entire sanctification is not nearly as widely used as some of the others, it clearly indicates what happens in the experience. What Wesley liked to call "inward sin"—the sin of the heart, out of which, as Jesus said, acts of sin come forth (see Mark 7:23)—is cleansed. Holiness people have been fond of pointing to one of the Beatitudes as support for this teaching where Jesus said, "Blessed are the pure in heart, for they shall see God" (Matt. 5:8).

13. *The Fullness of the Blessing*

This term is similar to *full salvation*—a designation widely used by the Salvation Army, which for some years now has been officially a member of the Christian Holiness Association. The "fullness" thought suggests a positive note.

Although the term might imply that the first work of grace

is somehow only partial, and not complete, in some sense this is true. The scriptural call is to "go unto perfection" (Heb. 6:1, KJV), and perfection suggests a full or complete salvation.

14. Sanctification

This term is similar to "holiness," discussed earlier. It is different, however, in that "holiness," popularly, has to do in part with what we do in order to live a devout life—the living out of our consecration to God's full will in our lives. While consecration is something we do by God's help, sanctification is something God does for us. *that we allow, request, hope for*

Consecration involves what we purpose to do with our talents, our money, etc. We consecrate them to God, and He sanctifies them in the sense of separating them from common uses to His uses. In this sense, in Old Testament times, the Levitical priesthood was sanctified, as were the Sabbath, tithes, sacrifices, etc.

The term "sanctification," has the advantage of being a word which most people would at least somewhat understand. And Holy Scripture itself often uses "sanctification" as referring to something God does in us. In Eph. 5:25-26, Paul says, "Christ also loved the church and gave Himself up for her; that He might sanctify her, having cleansed her by the washing of water with the word." Scripture customarily uses "sanctification" instead of "entire sanctification," only once expressly using what suggests the latter term (1 Thess. 5:23).

15. Entire Sanctification

All things considered, "entire sanctification" is perhaps the most preferable designation for Wesleyanism's distinctive emphasis.[9] Among the points in its favor are: (1) it is widely

---

9. The books with "entire sanctification" in the title are: S. L. C. Coward, *Entire Sanctification* (Chicago: Christian Witness Co., 1928); John Hunt, *Entire Sanctification: Its Nature, the Way of Its Attainment, Motives for Its Pursuit* (London: John Mason, 1860); W. Jones, *The Doctrine of Entire Sanctification* (Philadelphia: National Association for the Promotion of Holiness, 1885); Paul Kindschi, *Entire Sanctification* (Marion, Ind.: The Wesley Press, 1964); C. W. Ruth, *Entire Sanctification* (Chicago: Christian Witness Co., 1903); C. B. Whitaker, *Entire Sanctification, a Second Work of Grace* (Grand Rapids: S. B. Shaw, Holiness Record Office, 1887); A. Zepp, *Progress After Entire Sanctification* (Chicago: Christian Witness Co., 1909).

used and widely understood; (2) John Wesley himself used it quite frequently and urged its use, establishing thereby a tradition within Methodism and the Holiness movement generally; and (3) it suggests the doctrine's most significant aspect: the cleansing away of original sin. This experience of entire sanctification is wrought by, or effected by, or occasioned by the baptism with the Holy Spirit.[10]

---

10. See *Manual, Church of the Nazarene* (Kansas City: Nazarene Publishing House, 1976), articles V and X of the Articles of Faith.

Chapter 4

Spirit Baptism in Scripture

Pentecost itself, and the later Pentecosts of Acts, were times when born-again believers received entire sanctification— the second work of grace. If those Pentecosts were not times of entire sanctification, then the history of the first three decades or so of the Early Church was written without reference to the second work of grace. In that case, several things would obtain.

Importantly, you would have Peter, John, Paul, and others writing Epistles that teach and urge entire sanctification during the very time when Luke records what they did—and Luke in his history would not be recording any interest on their part in a second work of grace. Take Paul, for example. You would have a schizophrenia in which on the one hand he was telling the Christians at Ephesus (and the nearby area) that Christ gave himself up for the church to sanctify her, having already regenerated her (Eph. 5:25-27; see also 1:13; 3:1 ff.; 5:18); yet when visiting the church, he would have shown no interest in their receiving a second work of grace.

If the Epistles of Paul and others had all been written after the decades of ministries recorded in Acts, a person who does not believe that the Pentecosts in Acts are times of entire sanctification could suggest that the writers only later came to believe in a second work of grace and that thus it is urged in the Epistles. However, Acts records what was happening right during the decades when at least almost all the Epistles were being written.

Another important problem we would have to answer is

How ? (handwritten)

that the early churches would not have been briefed on entire sanctification during the years when they were being founded, but only later. The churches would have been founded and ministered to for a number of years, and then, out of the blue, the leaders would for the first time have introduced a brand-new, surprise teaching: that of entire sanctification. Not only would this imply that the second grace is not very important, but it would have been exceedingly poor strategy.

Instead, all through Acts, believers are led into a second work of grace through being baptized with or filled with, or through receiving, the Holy Spirit. We shall note a number of specific instances of this.

A. *Two Works of Grace at Samaria*

The revival at Samaria, described in Acts 8:1-25, is perhaps the Gibraltar of two-works-of-grace teaching. Even when compared with First Thessalonians, it is probably somewhat more unanswerably two-works-of-grace. The account of this event is most clear, on this matter of twoness, firstness and secondness, conversion and then a second work of grace. In Scripture, generally, as in nature itself, God's revelation is in spread-out, panoramic fashion, requiring theology to do for it what the physical sciences do for spread-out nature. In Acts 8, this is not so. It is as though we have already had a two-works-of-grace theologian doing his technical kind of work.

Luke tells us that Philip, who had been ordained only as a deacon to take care of more mundane matters so that the Twelve could have more time to preach (Acts 6:1-6), "went down to the city of Samaria and *began* proclaiming Christ to them" (Acts 8:5). He had been set aside, with six others, to be a waiter, to "serve tables" (Acts 6:2), but he was one early Christian who did considerably more than he was assigned to do. Times were tough, because Christians were being perse- cuted in an all-out, programmed assault, and they scattered out from Jerusalem. Times like that have often elicited the really committed services of Christ's people, and it was so for this "full of the Spirit" (Acts 6:3) deacon. He was popular as a preacher, for "the multitudes with one accord were giving attention to what was said by Philip" (Acts 8:6). People were being healed physically, and helped in other ways as well.

Requirement (handwritten, right margin)

Many people believed on Christ (were converted, that is) and received water baptism (Acts 8:12). The word got back to Jerusalem, and Luke tells us, further:

> When the apostles in Jerusalem heard that Samaria had received the word of God, they sent them Peter and John, who came down and prayed for them, that they might receive the Holy Spirit. For He had not yet fallen upon any of them; they had simply been baptized in the name of the Lord Jesus. Then they *began* laying their hands on them, and they were receiving the Holy Spirit (Acts 8:14-17).

As clearly as words can make it, then, they earlier believed, and were baptized in water in the name of Christ; and quite later, after the apostles had arrived, they received the Holy Spirit—"for He had not yet fallen upon any of them."

B. *Paul's Conversion*

While some feel that Paul was not converted out on the road to Damascus, but three days later when Ananias visited him that he might be filled with the Spirit, the interpretation of holiness scholars is that Paul was converted at the earlier time and that therefore being filled with the Spirit at the house of Ananias was subsequent to his justification.

1. Something revolutionary happened to Saul out there on the Damascus road. It was so revolutionary that Saul made a complete turnaround—from Christianity's main persecutor to being commissioned as a representative of his former enemy, Christ.

There were also outward manifestations of this revolutionary change. We read that "suddenly a light from heaven flashed around him" (Acts 9:3) and Paul "fell to the ground" (v. 4). The risen Christ, whom Paul had never seen in the flesh, appeared to him in a most miraculous fashion and held conversation with him. This was a conversion experience there and then —not later on Straight Street at Judas's house in Damascus, but on the Damascus road. We have been fond of saying that people need a "Damascus road" experience, by which we mean conversion. Of numerous commentators checked, almost none of them, whatever their own doctrinal stance, take the position that Paul's conversion did not occur on the Damascus road.

2. This zealous Pharisee—who breathes out threatenings,

who holds letters authorizing him to hunt out Christians at faraway Damascus and bring them bound to Jerusalem for trial—is called out there on the road to preach Christ. His call does not happen after Ananias gets there, but has already happened. The Lord said to Ananias: "Go, for he is a chosen instrument of mine, to bear My name before the Gentiles and kings and the sons of Israel" (Acts 9:15). Paul is not only an "instrument," but he is a "chosen instrument." The word for "chosen" is *ekloges,* which has strong salvation overtones. It is used in Rom. 11:5-7 concerning the remnant who enjoy God's grace.

3. Paul twice calls Christ *kurie* ("Lord," Acts 9:5; 22:8). Paul might have, at that early moment in the conversion experience, used *kurie* as simply a way of addressing an authority figure. Paul may be merely asking who He is ("Who art Thou, Lord?").

But in the other instance, Paul is reporting what had happened on that earlier occasion. He has already submitted to this "Lord." So he asks with even fuller meaning, "What shall I do, Lord?" Interestingly, the form in which it appears in both these places *(kurie)* is identical to the form used by the "full-fledged Christian," Ananias, who in Acts 9:10, in full obedience, says: "Behold, *here am* I, Lord."

4. Still more significant as supportive of the view that Paul was converted on the roadside, is that, as Ananias approaches Paul, he calls him "brother." We read, "Ananias departed and entered into the house, and after laying his hands on him said, 'Brother Saul, the Lord Jesus . . . has sent me'" (Acts 9:17). The suggestion of some that this use of "brother" denotes only Jewish kinship is too much. It robs the expression of its evangelical beauty. On the basis that Paul is already a Christian, Ananias is telling Paul, at the outset, that he considers him to be a fellow Christian believer. Paul needed to hear of that kind of acceptance, too, because he had been the chief mogul on the opposite side.

5. If Ananias had gone to Paul in order to help him to become converted, to be justified, to believe, to become a Christian, why do the accounts not use "conversion language"? Ananias says that Christ had sent him "so that you may regain your sight, and be filled with the Holy Spirit" (Acts 9:17). Ac-

tually, we are told only that Paul received his sight, and not that he was indeed filled with the Spirit as well. But later we read that Paul was at some time "filled," for it is said that "Saul, filled with the Holy Spirit, fixed his gaze upon him [Elymas]" (Acts 13:9).

6. In Paul's report of his conversion in Acts 22 he quotes Ananias as saying to him: "Now why do you delay? Arise and be baptized, and wash away your sins, calling on His name" (v. 16).

The reference here is to water baptism, not in order that it might wash away his sins (for water baptism itself does not do that), but in order that, by water baptism, he might symbolize the washing away of his sins that has already occurred. By water baptism, also, as a believer, he would be openly, by an extremely significant ritual act, witnessing to all and sundry that he was a Christian.

C. *The Case of Cornelius*

It must be admitted that Luke does not make it altogether clear that Cornelius is already a Christian when, upon him (and other Gentiles) "the gift of the Holy Spirit is poured out" (Acts 10:45). Yet the evidence is considerable on the side of the view that he was.

1. Cornelius is devout. Cornelius is said in Acts 10:2 to have been *eusebes,* which means "reverent; pious, devout, religious."[1] Another way of translating this word is "godly." It is the same word that is used in 2 Pet. 2:9 for "the godly" whom "the Lord knows how to rescue . . . from temptation." They are the opposite from "the unrighteous." It is a cognate of the word, *eusebeia,* that is used for the "godliness" of Paul and other Christians where Paul urges Timothy to pray for "all who are in authority" so that "we may lead a tranquil and quiet life in all godliness" (1 Tim. 2:2). This latter form of the word also appears in 1 Tim. 4:8 where it is used to denote what will put a person in good stead for the life to come. Paul says that this "godliness is profitable for all things, since it holds promise for the present life and *also* for the *life* to come."

---

1. *The Analytical Greek Lexicon* (New York: Harper and Brothers, n.d.), p. 176.

In an adverbial form, *eusebos,* it describes anyone who is decidedly "in Christ Jesus." Paul writes: "Indeed, all who desire to live godly in Christ Jesus will be persecuted" (2 Tim. 3:12). So while a form of the word appears in 1 Tim. 5:4 in reference to the practice of "piety" toward one's family, and while it is used in Acts 17:23 of the "worship" of people toward "an unknown God," its use in reference to Cornelius corroborates the view that he is a Christian believer—albeit, without very much correct understanding.

It is interesting that no one questions Ananias's being a true Christian, who was to Paul what Peter was to Cornelius— one sent of God to help. Ananias is called a "disciple" in Acts 9:10, a *mathetes,* which is the singular of the same word used to describe the people found by Paul at Ephesus (Acts 19:2). More than that, and specifically to our point here, another special description of Ananias is that, like Cornelius, he was "devout" (Acts 22:12). The word here for "devout" is *eulabes,* slightly different from *eusebes,* used of Cornelius in Acts 10:2. But, if anything, there is less that is distinctively Christian in the uses of *eulabes* than in the uses of *eusabes.* It happens, too, that Cornelius's devoutness is not qualified. He is simply "a devout man" (Acts 10:2). Ananias's devotedness is qualified, for he is described as "a man who was devout by the standard of the Law" (Acts 22:12).

Another parallel between Cornelius and Ananias is that both men are said to have been spoken well of by Jews. But Ananias had the goodwill of only the Jews at Damascus, whereas Cornelius had the goodwill of the whole Jewish nation. Of Ananias it is said that he was "well spoken of by all the Jews who were in that place" (Acts 22:12). Of Cornelius, Luke says that he was "a righteous and God-fearing man well spoken of by the entire nation of the Jews" (Acts 11:22).

2. *Cornelius is righteous.* When Cornelius is called "righteous" in Acts 10:22, the word used is *dikaios,* which is a much stronger suggestion that he is a Christian believer. It is a cognate of *dikaiosune,* the regular word used for justification in the New Testament. This very word, with the definite article, *ho dikaios,* the Just One, is even one of the distinctive titles of Christ in this same book (Acts) at 3:14; 7:52; and 22:14. It is one of the New Testament's special words for what God him-

self is, "just," and for what He makes us into by "faith in Jesus" (Rom. 3:26).

3. Other supportive factors:

a. Cornelius "feared God with all his household" (Acts 10:2), which means that he reverenced God and saw to it that his family and helpers did also.

b. He "gave many alms to the *Jewish* people" (Acts 10:2). This would of course not constitute him a believer, but would be an exemplary quality of a believer's life.

c. He "prayed to God continually" (Acts 10:2), which would be corroborative of his being devout and righteous.

d. He is wide open to God's will in his life, as is evidenced by his sending for Peter and by his implied willingness to do whatever the apostle suggested.

e. God gives him the special "vision," and the visit and ministry of an "angel" (Acts 10:3-7).

f. Just before the Spirit falls on Cornelius, Peter seems to be assuring him that he has already received forgiveness. Peter says to him: "Of Him [Christ] all the prophets bear witness that through His name every one who believes in Him has received forgiveness of sins" (Acts 10:43).

g. Further, Cornelius has already been "cleansed" by God. The reference is both to "unclean" animals, and to Cornelius as he was when Peter first learned about him. Luke tells us: "A voice from heaven answered a second time, 'What God has cleansed, no longer consider unholy'" (Acts 11:9). Peter could hardly get this through his thickened prejudices, so it had to be repeated "three times" (Acts 11:10).

h. And importantly, if he is not already forgiven of his sins, what is wrong here with our gracious God? If wayfaring people, though completely empty-headed, need not err in coming to God, why has this "God-fearing" man erred so badly as not to be justified, with all his seeking of and openness toward God? And if God is not willing that any should perish, but that everyone will come to repentance, why would He be holding this repentant seeker off from justifying grace? He may have lacked theological understanding, but at heart he was converted.

4. The aorist participle in 11:17, *pisteusantes,* translated "having believed," or "when we believed," in the minds of

some exegetes implies that Pentecost would be the time when Peter and others "believed," or were converted; and similarly that Cornelius's being baptized with the Holy Spirit was the time when he believed. The KJV reads, "Forasmuch then as God gave them the like gift as he did unto us, who believed on the Lord Jesus Christ; what was I, that I could withstand God?" Likewise the RSV reads, "If then God gave the same gift to them as he gave to us when we believed in the Lord Jesus Christ . . ." The NIV is similar: "So if God gave them the same gift as he gave us who believed in the Lord Jesus Christ . . ."

But the NASB, often much more careful to follow the Greek, translates it in the way aorist participles are normally to be rendered: in such a way that Pentecost happened *after* the 120 had believed, and in such a way that the Spirit's falling upon Cornelius was *after* he had believed. The NASB reads, "If God therefore gave to them the same gift as He *gave* to us also after believing in the Lord Jesus Christ, who was I that I could stand in God's way" (Acts 11:17).

One supposes that a given interpreter's basic theology often intrudes itself, as here. If an interpreter who does not believe that the Spirit baptism is subsequent to justification comes across an aorist participle which suggests that it is, he conveniently says that in the passage in question the aorist participle happens to be the much more rare coincidental aorist. In this view the participle expresses action which takes place at the same time as that of the main verb.

5. The Reference to Repentance. We read in Acts 11:18, "Well then, God has granted to the Gentiles also the repentance *that leads* to life." This verse is used to support the view that Cornelius was converted only after the Holy Spirit had fallen upon him. But it should be remembered that this was said a long time after the event. Peter is on the carpet about participating in gospel work among Gentiles. They are not speaking specifically about Cornelius's being baptized with the Spirit. They are criticizing Peter because he shared Christ with the "uncircumcised" and "ate with them" (Acts 11:3). It is not easy for this to seep through their prejudices even as it had not been easy in Peter's own case.

They are not so much worried about a second work of grace being extended to Gentiles, as they are about the gospel going to these uncircumcised people at all. If they could grant them the privilege of conversion, they would not have any problem about their getting in on the brand-new thing of a personal Pentecost. They are therefore not talking about Cornelius's baptism with the Spirit, but, more basically, about the gospel of God's forgiving grace going to a Gentile.

When they "quieted down" (Acts 11:18), they finally got around to saying: "Well then, God has granted to the Gentiles also the repentance *that leads* to life" (Acts 11:18).

While some holiness writers do not believe that Cornelius was a Christian until Peter visited him, they nevertheless hold that he was justified prior to the time when the Holy Spirit fell upon him in baptismal fullness.[2] Possibly supportive of this is the interpretation of the word "saved" in Acts 11:14, which they equate with "converted." The angel tells Cornelius, "Send to Joppa, and have Simon . . . brought here; and he shall speak words to you by which you will be saved" (Acts 11:13b-14). However, though cognates of *sodzo,* for "saved," are found as equivalents of conversion (as in Mark 16:16; Acts 2:21 and 16:31; Rom. 5:10 and 10:13), it is also used more widely as a synonym of the more inclusive term, *redemption.* One such passage is Matt. 10:22, where we read, "It is the one who has endured to the end who will be saved." (See also Matt. 24:13; Mark 13:13.)

In any case, the evidence is that Cornelius was a justified man before his baptism with the Spirit.

D. *The Second Grace at Ephesus*

Acts 19:1-7 is not as incontestably "two-works-of-grace" as Acts 8:1-25 is, but it is almost as clearly so. It describes how Paul found at Ephesus certain baptized disciples who had not

---

2. See Ralph Earle, Exegesis in "The Acts of the Apostles," *The Evangelical Commentary* (Grand Rapids: Zondervan Publishing House, 1959), pp. 136-37, 154; also Earle's exegesis in the *Beacon Bible Commentary* (Kansas City: Beacon Hill Press of Kansas City, 1965), 7:382, where he refers to Adam Clarke in support. In *Meet the Early Church* (Kansas City: Beacon Hill Press of Kansas City, 1959), pp. 49-50, Earle writes: "Cornelius and his companions were so completely receptive to the message that when they heard about believing in Jesus they immediately did so and were saved. But their hearts were so hungry for all of God's will, and so surrendered to Him that they were soon filled with the Holy Spirit in the same service."

as yet received the Holy Spirit, and who then received the Spirit.

On several bases, the Holy Spirit's coming upon them was subsequent to their conversion.

1. Paul calls them disciples *(mathetais),* a customary word for Christian believers. If it meant that they were disciples of anyone else, and not of Christ, that specific would have been mentioned.

2. They had already believed. Paul asked the Ephesian disciples, "Did you receive the Holy Spirit when you believed?" (Acts 19:2). Again, we have an aorist participle, *pisteusantes,* "having believed" (or, "when believing"). On the basis of what is customary with an aorist participle (that the action it expresses takes place prior in time to the action of the main verb of a sentence), this would read, "Having believed, did you receive the Holy Spirit?" Or, "After you believed," did you receive Him? The King James version translates it: "Have ye received the Holy Ghost since ye believed?"—not bad for a group of Calvinistic translators!

Whether or not one renders the passage in the way the aorist participle warrants, the two-works-of-grace meaning is present. For, after all, they had believed, and yet they told Paul they had "not even heard whether there is a Holy Spirit" (Acts 19:2).

3. Also, it is the believers at Ephesus who are called brethren in Acts 18:27, where we read that "the brethren encouraged him [Apollos]." It does not take much acquaintance with the New Testament to know that "brethren" is a term frequently used for Christians.

4. Luke tells us that "they were baptized in the name of the Lord Jesus"[3] (Acts 19:5). This had been by water. And his next words are: "When Paul had laid his hands upon them, the Holy Spirit came on them" (Acts 19:6). To be candidates for

---

3. Baptism in the name of the whole Trinity was not practiced in Acts. It is done only in "the name of Jesus." Matthew's Gospel, which gives the Trinitarian formula (28:19), had not yet been written. After it was written and disseminated, baptisms were done with the Trinitarian formula—an almost universal practice throughout Christian history.

water baptism, they would have repented, as the account implies, and they would have been believers, as the account says they were. After repenting and believing, then they were baptized. It was after their baptism[4] that the Holy Spirit "came on them." Receiving the Holy Spirit here (in the usual sense of that in Acts), is subsequent to believing on Christ.

E. *Paul's Reference in Romans 4*

The apostle Paul not only says in Romans 4 that Abraham in Old Testament times was justified, but he uses Abraham as an illustration of how anybody can be justified. William Greathouse says that "in Abraham's faith we see the *model* of Christian justification."[5] Paul says, "'Abraham believed God, and it was credited to him as righteousness'" (Rom. 4:3, NIV). He is here quoting Gen. 15:6, which also states that Abraham was justified or righteous. Paul does not seem to know anything about the dispensationalism which separates the pre-Pentecost people from justification by faith, because he uses Abraham as an illustration of how one is justified.

Paul says of Abraham, "He is the father of all who believe but have not been circumcised, in order that righteousness might be credited to them" (Rom. 4:11, NIV). Paul is saying that circumcision does not matter very much, but that to have faith is what is crucial. He sees no chasm between Abraham's time and those post-Pentecostal times. He is saying that in all times people have been justified, and that it has been by faith, and not by observing works (Rom. 4:4) nor by observing the law (Rom. 4:15).

Paul knows, of course, that, when he was writing the Romans epistle, people were to "believe in him who raised Jesus our Lord from the dead" (Rom. 4:24, NIV). But his point is that Abraham and his readers were also justified by faith and

---

4. This is the order in Acts 8: believing, baptism in water, then baptism with the Spirit. This is the usual New Testament order, although it is not always this clear (as, for example, in Paul's case). The proximity, time-wise, between believing in Christ and water baptism, all through Acts, would suggest that present-day holiness churches are perhaps too neglectful of this sacrament. Probably a certain liberality over the mode of baptism and over the "when" (infant or believer) has contributed to this lack of emphasis upon it.

5. William M. Greathouse, "Romans," *Beacon Bible Expositions* (Kansas City: Beacon Hill Press of Kansas City, 1975), p. 70.

not by works. It is elementary that people were justified before Pentecost.

F. *John's Gospel Is Corroborative*

According to the Gospel of John, many people enjoyed the blessings of justification prior to Pentecost. While it should be admitted that this Gospel was written long after Pentecost, so certain observations John makes do not apply to the pre-Pentecostal time, there is much which suggests that people enjoyed what we mean by the first work of grace prior to Pentecost. And much of this has to do with the period even prior to the Crucifixion and Resurrection.

It is possible that when Jesus said to Philip, "Follow me" (1:43), and Philip responded, it was like a conversion. Much more significant is Jesus' urging upon Nicodemus the new birth in chapter 3. Jesus says to him, "Unless one is born again, he cannot see the kingdom of God" (v. 3). Jesus does not tell him that he must wait with this matter of being born again until after Pentecost, or even until after His death and resurrection. He even seems to chide Nicodemus for not being born again right then because He says: "You do not receive our witness" (v. 11).

This Gospel also speaks much about eternal life, which is a synonym of justification or conversion. Jesus says, "He who believes in the Son has eternal life" (3:36). It is received when one "believes," which is one of the New Testament's ways of saying what one does in order to receive forgiveness or justification. It is a counterpart of the noun "faith"—so often used by the apostle Paul to denote what is necessary to obtain justification (see Rom. 5:1, for example).

Soon Jesus tells His disciples (which, incidentally, is also a word used for those who have believed) that the "fields" right at the time "are white for harvest" (4:35), without waiting for the Crucifixion or Pentecost. And He uses the present tense in saying, "Already he who reaps is receiving wages, and is gathering fruit for life eternal; that he who sows and he who reaps may rejoice together" (4:36). Then three verses later, he speaks of the many Samaritans who "believed" (4:39) because of the woman's witness. Was this not regeneration, the new birth, conversion which took place in their lives?

And how could regeneration be more clearly suggested than when Jesus later says, using the present tense, "For this is the will of my Father, that every one who beholds the Son, and believes in Him, may have eternal life, and I myself will raise him up at the last day" (6:40)? Then Jesus adds, "Truly, truly, I say to you, he who believes has eternal life" (6:47).

Numerous other references could be cited such as the story of the man healed of blindness who believes and begins to worship Jesus (c. 9); Christ's extended prayer for His disciples in chapter 17 in which He calls them "mine," and asks that the Father would "keep them" (not regenerate them) and further states that "they are not of the world"; Christ's added plea, "I do not ask in behalf of these alone, but for those also who believe in Me through their word" (17:20); and Thomas's confession on that post-Resurrection occasion: "My Lord and my God" (20:28).

The prayer of our Lord, "Sanctify them in the truth; Thy word is truth" (17:17), was answered at Pentecost. The word for "sanctify" is in the aorist tense, which would suggest the kind of punctiliar event that Pentecost was, being the time when they received the baptism with the Holy Spirit. This is a use of "sanctify" as meaning "make holy," in the sense of cleansing them, and would fit both the "and fire" of the Matt. 3:11-12 reference to the coming Pentecost, and the Acts 15:8-9 description of Pentecost as a time when the peoples' hearts were "purified."

G. *The Synoptics Are Supportive*

The Synoptic Gospels also teach that the first work of grace is possible before Pentecost. In these Gospels also, people receive the forgiveness of sins; they repent and believe; their lives become different and commissioned.

1. Matthew has many references indicating justification was possible prior to Pentecost. The ministry of John the Baptist by the Jordan is the starting point. The people who repented and were baptized under this man's preaching of repentance were believers, and were baptized as a witness to their faith. Further, they were enjoined to "bring forth fruit in keeping with *your* repentance" (4:8). Actually, he told them he was offering a first step in redemption, baptizing them in water,

and that Jesus himself, later, would offer a further stage in redemption, baptizing people with the Holy Spirit. He said, "As for me, I baptize you in water for repentance, but He who is coming after me is mightier than I, and I am not *even* fit to remove His sandals; He Himself will baptize you with the Holy Spirit and fire" (3:11-12).

It is more than a "half-way covenant" gospel, also, that Jesus himself preaches. Its demand, also, is for repentance: "Repent, for the kingdom of heaven is at hand" (4:17). People who accept this repentance He calls "salt," and "the light of the world" (5:13-14). Jesus gives them instructions, as insiders, who are to "love" their "enemies" (5:44), as He says, "in order that you may be sons of your Father who is in heaven" (5:45).

A paralytic was justified when Jesus said, "My son, your sins are forgiven" (Matt. 9:2). And people could become "converted," for we read, "Truly I say to you, unless you are converted, and become like children, you shall not enter the kingdom of heaven" (Matt. 18:3).

2. Mark and Luke add further support to pre-Pentecost conversion, some of the instances being already given in Matthew.

One which is distinctive to Luke is related to the sending out of the "Seventy." Jesus says to them, "Do not rejoice in this, that the spirits are subject to you, but rejoice that your names are recorded in heaven" (10:20)—a strong suggestion of justification. (See Rev. 20:15, "If anyone's name was not found written in the book of life, he was thrown into the lake of fire.")

On all these bases, then, from Acts and other areas of Scripture, it came to be taught, in the Holiness movement, that entire sanctification is "wrought by the baptism with the Holy Spirit" as a second work of grace subsequent to justification.

Chapter 5

The Holiness Movement
and Spirit Baptism

For over 100 years in America's Holiness movement, virtually all its authors have taught that the baptism with (or "of") the Holy Spirit is that instantaneous occurrence by which entire sanctification is wrought. Supportive of this, Leo Cox writes:

> It has been a quite general teaching among holiness advocates that Pentecost, or the baptism of the Holy Spirit, is identical with the gift given at entire sanctification. C. E. Brown understands the coming of the Holy Spirit upon the Church in New Testament times as an experience only for the believer. He explains a number of scriptural accounts in that manner. All who received the Holy Ghost were already initially "saved" persons. In a second crisis of salvation, the believer is baptized with the Holy Spirit, at which time the heart is purified by faith (Acts 15:9). Most of the writers in the modern holiness movement who follow the Wesleyan tradition are in substantial agreement with this position. In all this investigation no one has been found in this tradition who objects to this identification, although all do not give it equal emphasis.[1]

This represents a change from John Wesley's view, however. He did not associate Pentecost with the second work of grace (entire sanctification), but rather with justification. He no doubt understood Pentecost to be associated with some kind of cleansing, according to his *Explanatory Notes upon the New Testament* at Matt. 3:11. Yet he did not identify the cleansing by its fires with the cleansing of entire sanctification.

---

1. Cox, *John Wesley's Concept of Perfection,* p. 123.

To Receive the fullness of the H. S.
blessing " ''
empowerment " ''
effusion (A. Clarke)

SANCTIFYING CLEANSING   OUTPOURING

The Holiness Movement and Spirit Baptism / 59

As late as in 1770, he chided those who referred to the second work of grace as "receiving the Holy Ghost." He said that others may do so, if they wished, but that it is "not scriptural, and not quite proper; for they all 'received the Holy Ghost,' when they were justified."[2] Much earlier, in 1744, he had written, "I assert that til a man 'receives the Holy Ghost,' he is without God in the world; that he cannot know the things of God, unless God reveal them unto him by the Spirit; no, nor have even one holy or heavenly temper, without the inspiration of the Holy One."[3]

Daniel Steele, a respected exegete and theologian who taught at Boston University, stated that he had counted some 26 terms used by Wesley as denoting entire sanctification, and that the baptism of or with the Holy Spirit was not one of them.[4] Leo Cox correctly observes, "This teaching of Wesley may appear strange to some who insist that the Holy Spirit is given subsequent to regeneration at the time of a 'second blessing,' but in this concept Wesley is at one with most Reformed teaching."[5]

In Wesley's *Explanatory Notes*, on Acts chapters 2, 8, 10, 11, and 19, where the Spirit baptism is reported by Luke, one will not find any indication whatever that he sees the Spirit baptism as associated with entire sanctification. He believed, for example, that although Cornelius was in a state of acceptance before God, he was not a "Christian" believer in the evangelical sense until Peter got to him. He also says that Paul's conversion was not really effected on the Damascus road, but three days later, when Ananias went to him and he was filled with the Spirit.[6]

---

2. See John Wesley, *The Works of the Rev. John Wesley* (Kansas City: Beacon Hill Press, n.d.), 12:416; 6:10-11.

3. *Ibid.,* 8:49. Actually, we receive the Spirit at conversion by being born of the Spirit (Rom. 8:9; John 3:5). But Scripture often uses "receiving the Holy Spirit" as a synonym of being baptized or fitted with the Spirit (e.g., Acts 19:2). Wesley does not distinguish between being born of the Spirit at conversion and being baptized with the Spirit at entire sanctification. I think this is the way to view Rom. 8:9 and Acts 19:2 as in agreement with each other.

4. Daniel Steele, *Steele's Answers* (Chicago: Christian Witness Co., 1912), pp. 130-31.

5. Cox, *John Wesley's Concept of Perfection*, p. 122. See also John Calvin, *A Compend of the Institutes of the Christian Religion*, ed. Hugh T. Kerr (Philadelphia: Presbyterian Board of Christian Education, 1939), pp. 89-90.

6. Wesley, *Works*, 9:93.

In his *Appeal to Men of Reason and Religion,* Wesley connects receiving the "Holy Ghost" with justification when he says, "I assert that 'till a man receives the Holy Ghost, he is without God in the world.'"[7]

Herbert McGonigle, in an article in the *Wesleyan Theological Journal,*[8] presents an excellent study on this matter. He shows from Wesley's *Notes,* certain letters and sermons, and his *Plain Account,* that Wesley says very little about the Spirit baptism, almost never even using the term, but if and when he does, he connects such biblical references with justification and not with entire sanctification.

Adam Clarke, the distinguished exegete of early Methodism, seems to have viewed the relationship between Pentecost and entire sanctification much as Mr. Wesley himself did, though there are some isolated passages that are different. These are strong enough for Leo Cox to observe: "Adam Clarke, a contemporary of Wesley, emphasized the work of entire sanctification as a 'great effusion of the Holy Ghost.'[9] Without question, he associated the work of purifying from all sin with the Pentecostal outpouring of the Holy Spirit."[10]

But one might ask why Clarke, in his comments on Acts 2:1-8 and on other passages in Acts, does not associate the baptism with the Holy Spirit with entire sanctification. Nor does he in his *Entire Sanctification,* published in book form separately as an extract from his *Christian Theology.* In his essay on "The Holy Spirit," however, there is this reference: "God promised his Holy Spirit to sanctify and cleanse the heart, so as utterly to destroy all pride, anger, self-will . . . and everything contrary to his own holiness. . . . He is also the sanctifying Spirit . . . and as such he condemns to utter destruction the whole of the carnal mind."[11]

With John Fletcher (1729-85), Wesley's close associate, we

---

7. *Ibid.,* 12:416.

8. Herbert A. McGonigle, "Pneumatological Nomenclature in Early Methodism," *Wesleyan Theological Journal,* 8 (Spring, 1973), pp. 61-72.

9. Cox, *John Wesley's Concept of Perfection,* p. 125. Cox here quotes Peters, *Christian Perfection and American Methodism,* p. 107.

10. *Ibid.* As a reference, Cox gives Adam Clarke, *The Holy Bible with a Commentary and Critical Notes* (New York: Abingdon Press), 5:682-83.

11. Adam Clarke, *Christian Theology,* ed. Samuel Dunn (New York: T. Mason and G. Lane, 1840), pp. 162-63.

have an eminent theologian who definitely moves toward linking the baptism with the Holy Spirit with entire sanctification. He has no problem with the fact that people were truly justified before Pentecost—even long before New Testament times. But more significantly, in his lengthy treatment of "Christian Perfection," as the last of his "Checks," one will find him linking the Spirit baptism with entire sanctification. But it must be said that this idea was not integral to the way he taught entire sanctification.

Fletcher seems, however, to have experienced it personally in this way without letting his inner spiritual experience work fully into his theology. Joseph Benson wrote in his biography of Fletcher that as the head of Trevecca college Fletcher was much interested in "this fullness of the Spirit."[12] In 1781 Fletcher entered into the experience of entire sanctification and described it quite as we might today. The testimony, which has appeared in various publications, was given at a sort of house prayer meeting Fletcher attended. He said that the Wednesday previously God had spoken to him through a part of Romans 6. He went on to testify:

> I . . . tell you all to the praise of his love I am freed from sin! Yes, I rejoice to declare it, and to bear witness to the glory of his grace, that I am dead unto sin. . . . I received this blessing four or five times before; but I lost it by not observing the order of God, who hath told us, 'With the . . . mouth confession is made unto salvation.'

Fletcher had prefaced this testimony by reading aloud from Acts 2, and had shown that "the day of Pentecost was only the opening of the dispensation of the Holy Ghost—the great promise of the Father." He had exhorted the others, "O, be filled with the Holy Ghost. . . . O my friends, let us wrestle for a more abundant outpouring of the Spirit."[13]

Fletcher, whom Wesley respected so much that Fletcher would have been Wesley's successor if he had not died earlier, corresponded with Wesley on this issue. He tried to prove to

---

12. See Joseph Benson, *The Life of the Rev. John W. de la Flechere,* pp. 152-53, quoted in Peters, *Christian Perfection in American Methodism,* pp. 216-17.
13. See *Guide to Holiness* (January, 1860), pp. 40-41, located in the Rare Book Room, the Library, Nazarene Theological Seminary, Kansas City, Mo.

Wesley the validity of associating the baptism with the Holy Spirit with entire sanctification, but Wesley was unconvinced.[14] It remained for the American Holiness movement to elucidate the teaching.

I. THE HOLINESS MOVEMENT: EARLY PERIOD

America's Holiness movement began at about the year 1835. That is the year when Phoebe Palmer received entire sanctification and began a lay ministry which made her one of the three or four chief early promoters of holiness teaching. For some four decades she conducted Tuesday holiness meetings at which many persons received the experience of entire sanctification, among them a number who became prominent leaders in the movement. She wrote books that went through many editions. She and her physician husband bought the *Guide to Holiness* magazine and it was issued until 1903—long after their deaths. They conducted evangelistic campaigns both in America and in Britain that were very effective.

The year 1835 is also the year that Oberlin College in Ohio began its educating of women as well as men for holiness ministry, including its social implementation. Particularly, they were abolitionist and what we now call feminist. They also fostered caring for the poor, including opposition to various forms of exploitation of the disadvantaged. Asa Mahan, a Presbyterian minister from Ohio, became its first president, and Charles G. Finney, its first professor of systematic theology. (For the first couple of years, Finney spent only six months a year at Oberlin and the other six months as pastor of his New York City congregation of antislavery and revivalist enthusiasts.) At this same time, Timothy Merritt and George Peck were widely influential as Methodists who stressed entire sanctification.

It is of special interest here to trace not just entire sanctification teaching, but the significant aspect that this second work of grace is effected by the baptism of or with the Holy Spirit.

---

14. See Donald W. Dayton, "The Doctrine of the Baptism of the Holy Spirit: Its Emergence and Significance," *Wesleyan Theological Journal,* 13 (Spring, 1978), p. 116.

Thomas Webb (handwritten annotation)

A. *Pre-Holiness-Movement Teaching*

A progenitor of Spirit-baptism teaching was Thomas Webb (1724-96), a captain of the British army who was converted through Mr. Wesley's preaching and who became licensed as a local preacher. Sent to Albany, N.Y., about 1766 to be in command of a barracks there, he heard of a Methodist society being formed in New York City, and visited it. He soon became "their most active preacher"[15] and ultimately was called "the first Apostle of Methodism in America."[16]

The following excerpt from a Pentecost Day sermon by Webb contains a statement of his teaching:

> The words of the text were written by the apostles after the act of justification had passed on them. But you see, my friends, this was not enough for them. They must receive the Holy Ghost *after* this. So must you. You must be sanctified. But you are not. You are only Christians in part. You have not received the Holy Ghost. I know it.[17]

In 1772-73 Webb had contact, in England, with Joseph Benson, during the time when Benson and John Fletcher were beginning to teach entire sanctification through the baptism with the Holy Spirit. He sought to secure Benson's services as a missionary to America.

During the early decades of Methodism in the United States, especially the earliest decades of the 19th century, certain British Methodists who taught in this way were read and followed. Adam Clarke was one of them, although as was noted earlier in this chapter, he did not teach Spirit-baptism entire sanctification in a pronounced way.

There was also Hester Ann Rogers, whose *Memoirs* and *Letters* were circulated widely in American Methodism in the early 1800s. She relates her struggle to receive entire sanctification as follows:

Prayer (handwritten annotation)

> Lord, cried I, make this the moment of my full salvation! Baptize me now with the Holy Ghost and the fire of

---

15. Matthew Simpson, ed., *Cyclopaedia of Methodism* (Philadelphia: Everts and Stewart, 1878), p. 906.

16. *Ibid.*

17. John A. Knight, "John Fletcher's Influence on the Development of Wesleyan Theology in America," *Wesleyan Theological Journal*, 1978, p. 23. See also Coppedge, "Entire Sanctification in Early American Methodism, 1821-1835," *WTS Journal*, 1978.

pure love: Now 'make me a clean heart, and renew a right spirit within me.' Now enter thy temple, and cast out sin forever. Now cleanse the thoughts, desires and propensities of my heart, and let me perfectly love thee.[18]

After quoting this, Allan Coppedge says, "Quite clearly in her mind the experience of the baptism of the Spirit was identical with that of full salvation, and the widespread distribution of her story cannot but have made American Methodists more ready to see an intimate connection between the two concepts."[19]

Perhaps most important of all is the wide circulation in America, at this time, of John Fletcher's *Last Check,* in which he taught Spirit-baptism entire sanctification—but without extensive elucidation.

Interestingly, at this time, some who were outside of Methodism began to pick up this teaching, especially two Presbyterian denominations. One of these was the Cumberland Presbyterian Church, which broke off from the main Presbyterian body, in Kentucky and Tennessee, in 1810. Merrill E. Gaddis, in his unpublished Ph.D. dissertation (1929) at the University of Chicago, says that in some ways they were only "semi-perfectionistic," calling theirs a "quasi-perfectionism."[20] Yet they seem to have been basically both Arminian and Methodist in doctrine. Gaddis says:

> Calvinistic predestination was never more completely set aside than by the evangelists of this denomination, nor can the present-day student detect any actual difference— from the standpoint of religious psychology and practical moral results—between the Cumberland "Paraclete baptism" and its empowerment on the one hand, and the Wesleyan second blessing or "entire sanctification" on the other.[21]

Gaddis further suggests that in these directions they had been influenced by frontier Methodism. He writes, "The Cumberland preachers sent out by this presbytery were Methodistic

---

18. See Thomas Coke, *The Experience and Spiritual Letters of Mrs. Hester Ann Rogers* (London: Milner and Somerby, n.d.), p. 14. Quoted in Coppedge, *WTS Journal,* 1978, p. 46.

19. Coppedge, *WTS Journal,* 1978, p. 46.

20. Merrill E. Gaddis, "Christian Perfectionism in America" (Unpublished Ph.D. dissertation, University of Chicago, 1929), p. 298.

21. *Ibid.,* pp. 297-98.

in their message and procedure, and constitute at once a testi-monial to the influence exerted by Methodist associates and by frontier demands."[22]

In this connection, Allan Coppedge says, "Gaddis reports that among Cumberland Presbyterians, whose theological dis-position was quite Arminian, there was a tendency to speak about sanctification in terms of the baptism of the Holy Spirit as early as 1814."[23] Coppedge adds: "B. W. McDonald in his *History of the Cumberland Presbyterian Church* is very em-phatic about the importance which the early leaders of that denomination attached to the doctrine and experience of Holy Ghost baptism."[24] He also quotes McDonald as saying, "Our fathers believed in an abiding baptism of the Holy Ghost as a distinctive blessing after conversion. . . . Of all the doctrines held . . . the one about this abiding baptism of the Holy Ghost was most esteemed by them."[25]

The Cumberland Presbyterians have survived, and have about 100,000 members, with at least one college and a sem-inary. J. O. McClurkan, whose holiness group merged with the Church of the Nazarene in 1915, was from this denomination.

Besides the Cumberlands, the New Light Presbyterians, organized in the same area in 1803, taught in this way.

B. Finney's Strategic Contribution

A major contribution to the teaching of Spirit-baptism entire sanctification was made by Pastor-Evangelist-Professor Charles G. Finney. He clearly taught this in articles and "let-ters" in the *Oberlin Evangelist* in 1839-40; and to some extent, in the 1847 and 1851 editions of his *Systematic Theology.*

The *Oberlin Evangelist,* issued from the newly founded Oberlin College in Ohio, published a series of five lectures by Finney on "The Promises," from May to July, 1839. In these lectures he begins by quoting numerous Old Testament prom-ises, including that in Ezek. 36:25-26: "Then will I sprinkle

---

22. *Ibid.,* p. 295.
23. Coppedge, *WTS Journal,* 1978, p. 35.
24. *Ibid.* This is p. 105 in McDonald. Cited by Gaddis, *"Christian Per-fectionism,"* p. 46.
25. *Ibid.*

clean water upon you, and ye shall be clean. . . . A new heart also will I give you, and a new spirit will I put within you."[26]

He also quotes certain commandments, and suggests that if we are to receive the promises, we must keep the commandments. His use of such expressions as "fullness," is viewed by some interpreters as "entire sanctification language."[27] The word "fullness" is used somewhat vaguely, however, so that it is not specifically equated with the second-blessing experience.[28]

It is significant to note that in these five lectures Finney does not ever clearly say that entire sanctification comes about through the baptism of the Holy Spirit. He comes close to this when he affirms that this grace is "wrought by the Holy Ghost," but that is not the same as saying it is wrought by the *baptism* of the Holy Ghost.

Shortly afterward, however, in his "Letters to Ministers of the Gospel," published in the *Oberlin Evangelist,* he writes clearly to this point. In one such letter, published May 6, 1840, he says several things which reveal his emerging views on this matter. "The baptism of the Holy Ghost," he writes, "is . . . universally promised . . . to Christians"; and "this blessing is to be sought and received after conversion." He says that new

---

26. Charles G. Finney, "The Promises No. 1," the *Oberlin Evangelist,* edited by an association (Oberlin, Ohio: R. E. Gillet & Co., May 22, 1839), I, 87.

27. See Smith, *WTS Journal,* 1978.

28. Perhaps I should mention, here, that even such phrases as "baptism of the Holy Spirit," and "outpouring of the Spirit," which sound as if they are references to what happens in entire sanctification, are not always such references, in Finney. By "outpouring" he sometimes seems to refer to revival refreshing. And early in his *Memoirs,* as he describes his conversion, in 1821, he uses "baptism of the Holy Ghost" to describe that experience. He says, "But as I turned and was about to take a seat by the fire I received a mighty baptism of the Holy Ghost. Without any expectation of it, . . . the Holy Spirit descended upon me in a manner that seemed to go through me, body and soul" (*Memoirs of Rev. Charles G. Finney,* written by himself [New York: A. S. Barnes and Co., 1876], p. 20). Timothy L. Smith says in the article referred to earlier, in the *WTS Journal,* that Finney did not receive entire sanctification until some three years after his 1839 and 1840 articles in which he begins to teach Pentecostal entire sanctification. I agree with Smith that this is what the *Memoirs,* also called the *Autobiography,* suggests, even if the language never makes such expressly clear. It is interesting that in what Smith calls that little-noticed testimony in the *Autobiography,* Finney does not once use the phrase "baptism of the Holy Ghost," which he uses in the same writing of his 1821 conversion. And it should be noted that he is an elderly man as he writes this, calling his conversion a "baptism of the Holy Ghost."

converts should be "baptized into the very death of Christ . . . and raised to a life of holiness in Christ." He also says, "I am fully concerned that pains enough are not taken, to lead one convert to seek earnestly the 'baptism of the Holy Ghost, after that he hath believed.'" And he confesses that his own "instruction to converts, in this respect, has been very defective."

Finney does teach Pentecostal entire sanctification quite clearly in these "Letters." We could wish, however, that he were more specific on the matter of cleansing from original sin.

It is interesting, also, that there is very little teaching of this sort in either the 1847 or the 1851 editions of Finney's *Systematic Theology.* In that major work, he implies it, but it does not get enmeshed into his systematic presentation of theology. He teaches that the promises of "sanctification" were fulfilled by the baptism of the Holy Spirit at Pentecost. As he discusses sanctification—by which he means the entire sanctification of believers—he says that "a promise of sanctification, to be of any avail to us, must be due at some certain time . . . : that is, the time must be so fixed . . . as to put us into the attitude of waiting for its fulfillment. . . . The promise of Christ to the Apostles concerning the outpouring of the Spirit on the day of Pentecost, may illustrate the meaning."[29]

In another area of *Systematic Theology,* still treating "sanctification," Finney implies, but does not say expressly, that to be "baptized with the Holy Spirit," which he here equates with receiving "the fullness of the Holy Spirit," is what makes us, in distinction from the Old Testament personages, "perfect." He writes: "They [the Patriarchs] did not receive the light and the glory of the Christian dispensation, nor the fullness of the Holy Spirit. And it is asserted in the Bible, that 'they without us,' that is without our privileges, 'could not be made perfect.'"[30] Here he implies that our being baptized with the Holy Spirit renders us "perfect"—evidently in the sense of the Christian perfection that he is discussing.

C. S. S. Smith's Theological Importance

While Finney was one of the most significant religious fig-

---

29. Charles G. Finney, *Lectures on Systematic Theology* (Oberlin: James M. Fitche, 1847), p. 210.
30. *Ibid.,* p. 386.

ures of the 19th century, most especially perhaps, as an evangelist, Stephen Sanford Smith was not well known at all. Yet Smith, on the teaching that entire sanctification is occasioned by the baptism with the Holy Spirit, was highly strategic. Prior to his time no one had ever taught that doctrine as clearly as he did, nor as nearly like it came to be taught in the Holiness movement by the end of the 19th century.

S. S. Smith was a Congregational minister who was born in 1797, and died in 1871. He sometimes edited various secular papers and, along with other pastorates, supplied a church in 1840-41 at Newton, Mass.[31] It was during this pastorate that he published a strategic article in *Guide to Christian Perfection* (January, 1841) entitled "Power from on High," based on Luke 24:49: "Tarry ye in the city of Jerusalem, until ye be endued with power from on high" (KJV).[32]

In this sermon, Smith says, "The one hundred and twenty who were baptized with the Holy Ghost on the day of pentecost, had previously been 'born of God.'"[33] He goes on to say, "Evidently the gift of the Holy Ghost here alluded to [in John 7:39], is the power from on high referred to in the text, and as evidently it was not regeneration."[34]

After saying that this gift of power was not "of inspiration," nor "of working miracles," he asks, "What, then, was the power from on high promised in the text?"[35] One thing he says it was, was this: "It was a measure and fulness of the divine influence as transformed the whole moral character of the recipients."[36] About this transformation he says, "Never was change wrought in men on earth more thorough, than that wrought in the fol-

---

31. See *Congregational Necrology*, 1873, pp. 321-23.

32. Actually, Editors Merritt and King include at the end of the Smith sermon an editorial note in which they say they published another article the previous year with the same teaching in it. They say, "We had an article of the same import in our first volume. But as it was of ordinary length, it was necessarily far less explicit than the foregoing." They go on to say of Smith's article, "Brethren, read it, and read it again. And let us obtain the 'power from on high' . . ."

33. S. S. Smith, "Power from on High," *Guide to Christian Perfection*, Timothy Merritt and D. S. King, editors (Boston: Published by T. Merritt and D. S. King, 32 Washington Street, D. Ela, Printed 1840-41), p. 147.

34. *Ibid.*, p. 148.

35. *Ibid.*, p. 150.

36. *Ibid.*

lowers of Christ by the baptism with the Holy Ghost."[37]

Smith lays a careful groundwork, before expressly stating that it is entire sanctification that he feels the disciples received at Pentecost. One thing he finally says, in a footnote, is this: "That the baptism with the Holy Ghost was thus a sanctifying power is evident from the words of Christ, John vii 38—'He that believeth on me, as the scripture hath said, from him shall flow rivers of living water.'" In the same footnote, Smith goes on to say, "Paul also assures us that this baptism was a sanctifying influence," and adds that a person thus becomes "'a sanctified vessel,'"[38] with "every power and faculty of his soul brought into sweet subjection to the will of God."[39] He says it produces "'perfect love.'"[40]

Later on, in the last point of the sermon, he says that "millions had been regenerated by the Spirit of God, previous to this gift of the Holy Ghost after Christ was glorified."[41] And he views this baptism also as an empowerment, saying that "power from on high was granted by this baptism."[42] He further says that Christ "designed that primitive power should continue with a believing people to the end of the world."[43]

Smith feels the urgency of his message. He says, "The only power, then, that can render the modern church what the ancient prophets predicted it should be, and what the primitive church was, is the *baptism with the Holy Ghost,* of which she is now evidently generally ignorant and destitute."[44]

No one prior to this time, on either side of the Atlantic, had ever elucidated entire sanctification by the Spirit baptism as well as this. Nor had anyone viewed it so similarly to the way the Holiness movement has taught it since around 1900. S. S. Smith's use of "with" shows that this is Christ's baptism, not now with water, but with the Holy Spirit. He thus keeps it Christological, which is what the New Testament does (see Matt. 3:11-12).

---

37. *Ibid.*
38. *Ibid.,* p. 152.
39. *Ibid.*
40. *Ibid.*
41. *Ibid.,* p. 154.
42. *Ibid.*
43. *Ibid.*
44. *Ibid.,* p. 161.

D. *Other Early Contributors*

Methodists Timothy Merritt and D. S. King, who jointly edited *Guide to Christian Perfection,* contributed greatly to the development of holiness doctrine by publishing many key articles and sermons. A few months prior to their publishing Smith's article, they had published a shorter article titled "Short Sermon—the Baptism of the Holy Ghost," written by "H. C.," who is Oberlin's Henry Cowles. The text for this sermon is Acts 1:5 (KJV): "'Ye shall be baptized with the Holy Ghost not many days hence.'" In this sermon, Cowles argues that the "blessings" promised in this baptism did not include "the grace of conversion, or regeneration." He says that "the Apostles were converted some years before." While he does not expressly state that this baptism accomplishes entire sanctification or Christian perfection, he argues that it produced "love" and fearless witnessing, and that it effected "a change more striking than even that of their first conversion." In another sermon at about this time, Cowles speaks of the Spirit's *"sanctifying agency,"* and of His *"purifying our hearts."*

Besides these two sermons by Cowles, the editors published about four letters and articles by a Presbyterian minister, Charles Fitch, who also basically taught Spirit-baptism entire sanctification.

George Peck wrote considerably in the area of Christian perfection, but nowhere does he give a sustained treatment of entire sanctification through the baptism with the Holy Spirit. Within a 34-page article on "Christian Perfection," however, where he discusses how Christian perfection is to be "attained," he says something which is at least rather express on the matter of Spirit-baptism entire sanctification: "It is especially indicated as the work of the Holy Spirit by being denominated the *baptism of the Holy Ghost, sanctification of the Spirit,* etc. This view of our authors [he means Fletcher and other Methodists] is, that the work is *effected* and *sustained by the direct agency of the Spirit of God upon the Soul.* "[45]

Methodism's Bishop Hamline wrote an extended testimony entitled "Baptism," first published in 1843 in the *Ladies' Re-*

---

45. George Peck, "Christian Perfection," *Methodist Quarterly Review,* edited by himself (New York: G. Lane and P. P. Sanford, 1841), Volume XXIII, Third Series, Volume I, p. 151.

pository (of which he was editor), and republished in *Guide to Holiness* in 1846. Couching his testimony in third-person language,[46] the bishop gave several pages to a careful recounting of his experience of entire sanctification which he said occurred by the baptism of the Holy Spirit.

E. Phoebe Palmer's Contribution

Phoebe Palmer—discussed earlier in this chapter, a lay Methodist evangelist and writer—by the mid-1850s came to view entire sanctification as effected by the Spirit baptism. She spent four years in Britain, roughly during America's Civil War years, and taught this aspect of holiness doctrine there, publishing reports of her work in *Guide to Holiness,* often as letters to her sister and others. In 1859, her letter from Newcastle says she had taught "the endowment of power, the full baptism of the Holy Ghost, as the indispensable, ay, *absolute* necessity of all the disciples of Jesus."[47] It should be said that Mrs. Palmer's contribution to the doctrine and experience of entire sanctification in a general way is much more significant than is her contribution to the specific matter that the second grace happens by Spirit baptism.

F. Asa Mahan's Strategic Significance

In 1862, Asa Mahan gave as lectures at Adrian College the material he published in 1870 as *The Baptism of the Holy*

---

46. This fits in with his urging much carefulness in testifying to entire sanctification, if one was to testify at all to this grace.

47. Quoted in Dayton, "Asa Mahan and the Development of American Holiness Theology," *WTS Journal,* 1974, p. 62. It is interesting that a book which became exceedingly popular at about this time does not teach Spirit-baptism entire sanctification—when, by its title, you might expect it to. I refer to *The Tongue of Fire,* by Englishman William Arthur, published in America in 1856 and finally translated into numerous languages. One would think, from the title, that the whole book will consist of an elucidation of this view. Even so, some of the language is here, and certain rudimentary indications of the view are found. One of the closest associations I could find is where Arthur writes, "But 'I will pour out my Spirit upon you,' 'I will sprinkle clean water upon you,' is language and thought familiar to all readers of the Bible." Arthur is more interested in the power of Pentecost than in the cleansing from original sin through that event. And the title of his book is in great part simply a literary expression. The title does not mean that Arthur is to treat Pentecost and what it means theologically. He is more interested in appealing to the reader's heart than in speaking to his intellect.

Ghost, which book was widely circulated and had major impact, partly in Britain and on the Continent (through translations), but mainly in America. It is a milestone book on this aspect of the doctrine of entire sanctification.

Mahan's main objective in his book is to show that the Spirit baptism is a second work of grace: that the proper candidates for it are believers. He emphasizes the empowerment aspect of Pentecost rather than its cleansing; but he also teaches, though barely, that it does cleanse from sin. He is unusual among holiness writers in making much of the Spirit's coming upon Jesus at the time of His baptism in water. This could not be to cleanse Jesus from sin—original sin. It was to empower Him for the ministry He was to set out upon.

Mahan believed also that Christ's breathing on His disciples and saying "receive the Holy Spirit" was fulfilled at Pentecost. He writes:

> When our SAVIOUR came to His disciples and breathed upon them, saying, "Receive ye the HOLY GHOST," He did so, not because there was any virtue in that breath, or in the mere words spoken, or because the "gift of the SPIRIT" was then to be conferred as He had promised. A considerable period intervened between the time of the events here recorded, and that of the Pentecostal baptism. These events occurred (see John 20:22) at the first meeting of CHRIST with His disciples after His resurrection; whereas the baptism of the Pentecost was quite forty days afterwards. What, then, was the object of our SAVIOUR in what He did and said? It was evidently this, to induce in their hearts that state of *waiting expectation* and *inward preparation* which are the necessary prerequisites to the reception of the all-crowning gift of GOD.[48]

He followed the position that at Samaria many were already converted, and that later the Holy Spirit came upon them. And regarding the "Ephesian Pentecost," he says:

> Paul did put this question to the twelve believers whom he met at Ephesus; namely, "Have ye received the HOLY GHOST since ye believed?" or, as some render the original, "Did ye receive the HOLY GHOST when ye believed?" Why did he put this, and not the other question equally pertinent, if this doctrine is true, in each case, to wit: "Have ye received the pardon of your sins since ye believed?" or, "Did ye receive the pardon of your sins when ye believed?"

---

48. Mahan, *Baptism of the Holy Ghost,* p. 60.

Had he held and taught the dogma that both blessings are always and at the same moment given the instant an individual believes, he would have been just as likely to have asked if one blessing had been received, as whether the other had been, and the inquiry would have been infinitely absurd in either case.[49]

Mahan believed, as most do today, that we do receive the Spirit at conversion, but not in His baptismal fullness. This is the way he interprets 1 Cor. 12:13, where we read, "By one Spirit we were all baptized into one body, whether Jews or Greeks, whether slaves or free, and we were all made to drink of one Spirit." He says, "The Holy Ghost had given the disciples 'repentance unto life,' and 'was with them' as a sanctifying presence, had made their bodies His temple, and had 'baptized them into one body,' prior to Pentecost."[50] But the reference to baptism, here, is to water baptism, not to Spirit baptism. Since no one comes to the Father except the Spirit draws him, we are as believers baptized in water, symbolizing the renouncing of our sins, by the Holy Spirit, who has helped us to turn to Christ.

Mahan had also noted what Rom. 8:9 says: that "if anyone does not have the Spirit of Christ, he does not belong to Him." Thus he says, speaking of Cornelius and his household, "They must have had 'the Spirit of Christ,' or they could not have been His."[51] We have the Spirit by being *born* of the Spirit, at conversion. We receive the Spirit by being *baptized* with Him, at entire sanctification.

As noted before, Mahan emphasizes Pentecost's empowerment and not its cleansing aspect. He does, however, refer more or less vaguely to its being a time of cleansing for the believer. He sees, for example, the prophecy in Ezekiel 36, about clean water being sprinkled upon us, as fulfilled by Pentecost.

G. J. A. Wood on Cleansing

J. A. Wood was much more Wesleyan on the doctrine of original sin than were Mahan and Finney. He taught that entire

---

49. *Ibid.,* pp. v-vi.
50. *Ibid.,* p. iv.
51. *Ibid.* It is widely understood that the Spirit of Christ is not Christ himself, but the Holy Spirit. The "of Christ" means "who proceeds eternally from Christ."

sanctification is wrought by the baptism with the Holy Spirit, and that it is an empowerment. But, more importantly, he affirmed that it is the time of our cleansing from sin. He was a long-time holiness evangelist, preaching in many of the camp meetings that had been begun to promote holiness within the denominations—especially, Methodism. In 1861, in his 32nd year, he first wrote his widely influential *Perfect Love.* In the preface of a revised edition published 20 years later, he was able to write:

> It is a pleasant item that after twenty years of reading, study and enlarged experience since the first writing, I find not an essential point to renounce, therefore my work has been to systematize, state more clearly, enlarge, make stronger and add other important items.[52]

Wood writes of "when the soul is baptized with the Holy Ghost, and sin is utterly destroyed, and love, pure, perfect love, fills the whole heart."[53] He also writes:

> The disciples, before the Pentecost, were Christians. They had been chosen out of the world; they were the servants and companions of Christ; they had preached Jesus and the resurrection; they had cast out devils, and they loved the Saviour, and had denied themselves, taken up their cross, and had followed him.[54]

There seemed to be at this time a groundswell toward viewing entire sanctification as being wrought by the baptism with the Holy Spirit. By 1885, it seems to have been almost universally agreed upon in the Holiness movement. In that year the General Holiness Assembly agreed upon a statement of faith on the doctrine of entire sanctification which viewed it as wrought by the baptism with the Holy Spirit. Young A. M. Hills, an Oberlin graduate, later to write significant books on entire sanctification, and a major systematic theology, wrote:

> We are now prepared to give a formal definition of sanctification or Scriptural holiness, which would probably be accepted by the three hundred teachers and preachers in the National Holiness Association of America . . . Entire Sanctification is a second definite work of grace wrought by the Baptism with the Holy Spirit in the heart of the believer

---

52. John A. Wood, *Auto-Biography of Rev. J. A. Wood* (Chicago: The Christian Witness Co., 1904), p. 105.

53. Wood, *Perfect Love,* p. 4.

54. *Ibid.,* p. 290.

subsequent to regeneration, received instantaneously by faith, by which the heart is cleansed from all corruption and filled with the perfect love of God.[55]

Of this, John Peters observes:

This definition had something of the force of an "apostles' creed" within the Holiness movement. It was limited as was that first great formulary to the specific issues in controversy and was effective to expose the uncertain and to rout the disaffected. This was the phraseology in which the doctrine was presented, and its strength lay in its intensity.[56]

H. Daniel Steele

The most scholarly and the most respected Holiness movement writer, no doubt, was Daniel Steele, founding president of Syracuse University, where he began, in the early 1870s, to urge the concept that the baptism with the Holy Spirit is what effects entire sanctification. Perhaps the most prolific writer of holiness books of his time, one of his earliest works was *Love Enthroned,* published in 1878. He authored a number of other holiness books through the 1890s. He became professor of New Testament Greek at Boston University 1884-93, and also taught systematic theology there.

In *Love Enthroned,* he vigorously teaches that the baptism with the Holy Spirit is what effects a real, "Methodist-like" entire sanctification. He says, "The conclusion is inevitable, that the baptism of the Holy Ghost includes the extinction of sin in the believer's soul as its negative and minor part, and the fullness of love shed abroad in the heart as its positive and greater part; in other words, it includes entire sanctification and Christian perfection."[57]

To Steele, one of the special "proofs" that the Spirit baptism is a "synonym for entire sanctification" is "Peter's incidental remark in Acts 15:9, that the Holy Ghost came to Cornelius and his house in his office as Sanctifier, 'purifying their hearts by faith.'"[58]

---

55. See A. M. Hills, *Scriptural Holiness and Keswick Teaching Compared* (Manchester: Star Hall Publishing Co., n.d.).

56. See Peters, *Christian Perfection and American Methodism.*

57. Daniel Steele, *Love Enthroned* (Appollo, Tenn.: The West Publishing Co., 1951), p. 66.

58. *Ibid.,* p. 67.

Steele has no problem about Cornelius. He says, "The reception of the Holy Spirit in his fullness presupposes their [the house of Cornelius] previous repentance unto life."[59] He goes on to say: "We understand that the baptism, the anointing, the fullness, the abiding, the indwelling, the constant communion, the sealing, the earnest, of the Holy Spirit, are equivalent terms, expressive of the state of Christian perfection."[60]

Steele gives various supports for the position that "before the day of Pentecost the apostles had experienced the new birth."[61] They were "branches," and were "clean," and "not of the world."

II. The Holiness Movement: Middle Period

The period from 1885 up to, but not including, holiness exegetes and theologians now living, can be considered the Holiness movement's middle period.

A. *Its Characteristics*

This middle period was a time when "Pentecostal" became widely used as almost a synonym for entire sanctification. "Pentecostal" got into the names of many of the new denominations that were formed. In 1907, some of these in the eastern United States merged with Phineas Bresee's holiness denomination of the West, and they all became known as the Pentecostal Church of the Nazarene. The word *Pentecostal* was also used in the names of periodicals. In 1897, the latter part of the name of *Guide to Holiness* ("and Revival Miscellany"), was changed to "and Pentecostal Life." Pentecostal meetings and Pentecostal testimonies and Pentecostal groups within local churches were the common subjects in holiness magazines. Unfortunately, in the teens of our century, "Pentecostal" became increasingly associated with tongues-speaking. This occasioned its being dropped in 1919 from the name of the Pentecostal

---

59. *Ibid.*, p. 68.
60. *Ibid.*, p. 70.
61. Daniel Steele, *Half-Hours with St. Paul* (Boston: The Christian Witness Co., 1895), p. 123.

Church of the Nazarene. Yet it was still often used in holiness literature.

During this middle period, numerous denominations, with their many colleges, were formed. It had been thought earlier that the holiness people should remain with their various denominations and try to be a leavening influence. Holiness associations were formed in many areas for such persons. Holiness camp meetings brought to them the various widely known holiness preachers and writers.

Finally, however, it was felt by many that to remain in denominations that did not really want them was not as advantageous for the spread of scriptural holiness as it would be to come out of the denominations and form new ones committed to holiness doctrine. For the most part, this meant to come out of Methodism, some of whose bishops, right at this time, were making official pronouncements against the holiness members. Peters comments: "Thus by 1900 the greater part of the outspoken advocates of holiness . . . had withdrawn or become encouraged to leave American Episcopal Methodism. The Holiness movement had fully entered the period of separation and sect formation."[62]

B. *Its Writers*

Phineas Bresee, founder of the Church of the Nazarene, which became, with its many mergers, by far the largest of these holiness denominations, taught that the Spirit baptism effects entire sanctification. William McDonald[63] and J. A. Wood, who both taught in this way, held a meeting for Bresee in 1886 at the Methodist church he pastored at Pasadena, Calif., and seem to have influenced him much.[64]

At the organizational meeting of the Church of the Nazarene in 1895, J. A. Wood conducted what became the first of

---

62. *Ibid.*

63. McDonald says that "purifying their hearts by faith" spoken of by Peter in describing what happened to Cornelius, was the Pentecostal work. See William McDonald, *Another Comforter; or, the Personal Mission of the Holy Spirit* (Boston: McDonald, Gill and Co., 1890), pp. 61-72; and his *Scriptural Way of Holiness* (Chicago: The Christian Witness Co., 1907), pp. 125-29.

64. See E. A. Girvin, *A Prince in Israel* (Kansas City: Pentecostal Nazarene Publishing House, 1916), pp. 87-94; Jones, *Perfectionist Persuasion*, pp. 97-98.

the annual holiness meetings. Numerous prominent National Holiness Association evangelists had already preached for Bresee and they convinced Bresee of the validity of this view. One of these evangelists, I. G. Martin, not as prominent as many of the others, wrote a small book in which he quotes Bresee as saying, "We rejoice that we live in the abiding Pentecost."[65]

As early as in 1894 Bresee contributed a chapter on "Baptism with the Holy Ghost" to a 425-page holiness symposium edited by William Nast and titled *The Double Cure.*[66] In it Bresee says, "It would not seem necessary to urge at length that these are the days of the Holy Ghost baptism.[67] He also says, "This baptism with the Holy Ghost imparts power to the soul,"[68] but goes beyond the thought of empowerment, to affirm that it is the time of heart purification. Bresee says:

> *It purified their hearts.* This, Peter clearly declares in the council at Jerusalem, telling them how God led him, and justified his going to Cornelius, a Gentile, by the fact that the Holy Ghost fell upon him and those gathered, as it did upon them in the beginning, and put no difference between them—"purifying their hearts by faith"—evidently declaring that the baptism of the Holy Ghost purifies the heart.[69]

It was the following year that Bresee started the Church of the Nazarene. The Church of the Nazarene was born with the baptism with the Holy Spirit on its lips.[70] For these people to preach that entire sanctification is wrought by a baptism has about it a special homiletical advantage. It brought the conceptual language of entire sanctification down into a concrete form that can be visualized and perhaps better understood.

Bresee's address to the 1903 Nazarene general assembly shows how significant to him this aspect of holiness doctrine was:

---

65. I. G. Martin, *Dr. P. F. Bresee and the Church He Founded* (Mansfield, Ill.: I. G. Martin, 1937), p. 44.

66. Phineas Bresee, "Baptism with the Holy Ghost," *The Double Cure,* ed. William Nast (Chicago: The Christian Witness Co., 1894).

67. *Ibid.,* p. 327.

68. *Ibid.,* p. 335.

69. *Ibid.*

70. Floyd T. Cunningham, In a term paper submitted for a Doctrine of Holiness class at Nazarene Theological Seminary.

> The fires of the Pentecost in which this church was born have not grown dim. . . . The sanctification of believers through the baptism with the Holy Ghost by our risen Lord, giving power to witness for Him, has not ceased. . . . There prevails among us everywhere the deep conviction that the dispensational truth is that Jesus Christ baptizes with the Holy Ghost, cleansing, filling and empowering. . . . The result is that our people live, mostly, in the Pentecostal glory.[71]

Numerous such "Pentecostal" references from Bresee's writings could be produced here, such as when he says in an editorial in the *Nazarene* on January 7, 1904:

> We live in the dispensation when Jesus Christ baptizes with the Holy Ghost, and when the conviction of sinners, and the empowering of believers to carry on the work of Jesus Christ in the world depends upon their having become subjects of this baptism. . . . The incoming of the Holy Spirit into our hearts [does] for us what He did for the disciples on the day of Pentecost, purifying our hearts by faith. . . . What every individual heart must have is the baptism of Jesus with the Holy Spirit.[72]

Bresee seems to have preferred "the baptism with the Holy Spirit" to the many other names then in use for entire sanctification.[73]

Talking in these same terms, William McDonald, associated with Bresee very early, says, "If the baptism of the Holy Spirit did purify the hearts of the first disciples from that depravity which lingered with and in them, even after they had been called, accepted, and commissioned of Jesus, then it may do the same thing for us. A Pentecost awaits us, as well as them."[74]

At about the same time, Dougan Clark, in his fine work, *The Theology of Holiness,* teaches similarly:

> "God which knoweth the hearts, bare them witness, giving them the Holy Ghost, even as He did unto us, and put no difference between us and them, purifying their hearts by faith." Evidently here the chief of the apostles gives us to understand that the giving of the Holy Ghost, and the purifying of the heart by faith, are co-instantaneous

---

71. See Girvin, *Prince in Israel,* p. 199.
72. *Ibid.,* p. 210.
73. *Ibid.,* pp. 234, 237, 249, 257, 258, 275.
74. McDonald, *Another Comforter,* p. 55.

and identical experiences. And if this be so, the Holy Ghost, who is a Divine person, and not a mere influence, must be the effective agent in purifying the heart, that is to say, it is He who by His Divine energy sanctifies us wholly.[75]

Early in the Holiness movement's middle period, E. F. Walker, who later became a Nazarene general superintendent, wrote *Sanctify Them,* based on Christ's prayer in John 17:17 and its fulfillment at Pentecost. He writes, "The prayer of Jesus Christ that His disciples might be 'sanctified truly' is the same as that of Paul for the Thessalonians that they might be 'sanctified wholly' (1 Thess. 5:23). That is, through-and-through sanctification—the whole spirit and soul and body—the entire being separated from all sin and united to God."[76]

Also typically "Holiness movement" in his understanding that entire sanctification comes through the baptism with the Holy Spirit was A. M. Hills.[77] Along with teaching it in many positive ways, he laments its neglect in "the leading Protestant denominations in America," and adds: "The real cause of our leanness is: 'The Neglect of Pentecost.' The followers of Christ have ceased all too generally to repair to the sacred chamber and seek with importuning prayer for the BAPTISM WITH THE HOLY GHOST."[78] Despite this, he felt that holiness doctrine had earned a certain respect. He writes, "The doctrine of a possible deliverance from sin through the baptism with the Spirit has earned respectful attention rather than contemptuous rejection."[79] He deplores the Oberlin-Keswick neglect of a

---

75. Dougan Clark, *The Theology of Holiness* (Boston: The McDonald and Gill Co., 1893), p. 165.

76. Walker, *Sanctify Them,* p. 65.

77. Hills was the first outstanding theologian of the Church of the Nazarene. Perhaps Finney and Hills and Wiley are the three most significant theologians of the Holiness movement's history. Hills was a student of Finney at Oberlin, and was long associated with Wiley in Nazarene work. Hills published his classic on holiness in 1897; and his *Fundamental Christian Theology: A Systematic Theology,* in 1931. The first has perhaps been the most widely used work on holiness by Nazarenes, being on the Home Study Course for ministers for so long. His work on systematic theology replaced Miley's *Systematic Theology* in that course for the 1932 and 1936 quadrennia, until the first volume of H. Orton Wiley's three-volume *Christian Theology* appeared in 1941.

78. A. M. Hills, *Pentecost Rejected and the Effects on the Churches,* (Cincinnati: Office of God's Revivalist, 1902), p. 5.

79. *Ibid.,* p. 13.

cleansing emphasis by suggesting, "There is a class of religious teachers who champion Pentecost, but belittle the experience. They commend the baptism with the Holy Ghost, but deny its efficacy to cleanse the heart from inbred sin."[80]

Also associating Pentecost with entire sanctification even as Bresee and Hills and others did was E. P. Ellyson, who writes, "The atonement has provided a further experience wherein there is full cleansing from the state of sin. This cleansing is a part of the work of the baptism with the Holy Spirit."[81] He shows here a weaning away from the Oberlin use of the expression "baptism of" instead of "baptism with" the Spirit, as most authors were showing by his time. He also shows, as in general the others also do by his time, that a real cleansing takes place, and not simply an empowerment—as Mahan and Finney talked about almost exclusively.

The major theologian of the Holiness movement, H. Orton Wiley, explains, "The baptism with the Spirit . . . must be considered under a twofold aspect: *first,* as a death to the carnal nature; and *second,* as the fullness of life in the Spirit."[82] He goes on to say, "Since entire sanctification is effected by the baptism with the Spirit, it likewise has a twofold aspect—the cleansing from sin and full devotement to God."[83] It is unusual that in his 1,468-page, three-volume *Systematic Theology,* Wiley devotes less than one page to "The Baptism with the Spirit," under that heading as such. Yet he frequently teaches entire sanctification by Spirit baptism elsewhere in his major work. In one of these references he says: "Nothing can be more evident than that the baptism with the Holy Ghost effects an internal and spiritual cleansing which goes far deeper than John's baptism. One was for the remission of sins, the other for the removal of the sin principle."[84] In this reference he also says, in distinction from Wesley, "This baptism is applicable to Christians only, not to sinners."[85]

80. *Ibid.,* p. 30.
81. E. P. Ellyson, *Bible Holiness* (Kansas City: Beacon Hill Press, 1952), p. 69.
82. H. Orton Wiley, *Christian Theology* (Kansas City: Beacon Hill Press, 1941), 2:324.
83. *Ibid.*
84. *Ibid.,* p. 444.
85. *Ibid.*

Like Hills, Ellyson, and so many others in the Holiness movement, even Wiley does not seem to realize that, in closely identifying entire sanctification with the baptism with the Holy Spirit, he was different from Wesley. This is assumed because Wiley discusses Wesley as though the great Methodist is in full agreement with him.[86]

S. S. White, who holds a high rank among holiness theologians, wrote extensively on the subject. In his *Five Cardinal Elements in the Doctrine of Entire Sanctification,* he gives as one of the "five" the baptism with the Holy Spirit. He says that entire sanctification and the Spirit baptism "are simultaneous—identical in time but not necessarily in meaning."[87] And he writes, "The efficient cause [a reference to Aristotle, for White was as much a philosopher as a theologian] of entire sanctification is the baptism of Jesus with the Holy Spirit."[88] (He was anxious that we did not say "of," but "with" the Spirit—so that it was Jesus' baptism and not that of the Holy Spirit himself. White was christological—not pneumatological, as the Oberlin school had tended to be.)

White viewed Cornelius as "a saved man" (Acts 10:2, 22) who later "received the baptism with the Holy Spirit" (Acts 10:44).[89] And he associated that Caesarean Pentecost with cleansing from sin, explaining, "When the Holy Spirit fell upon Cornelius, his heart was purified or sanctified" (Acts 15:8-9).[90]

Concerning Christ's high priestly prayer in John 17, he writes: "Pentecost as described in Acts 2 is the answer to the great high priestly prayer of Jesus for the sanctification of His disciples (John 17). If such were not the case, we would have no reason to believe that Christ's prayer was ever answered."[91] No doubt one of the reasons why White would have looked for it to be answered at a given time, in a specific event, is because "sanctify," in the prayer, is in the punctiliar aorist tense.

---

86. *Ibid.,* pp. 455 ff.

87. Stephen S. White, *Five Cardinal Elements in the Doctrine of Entire Sanctification* (Kansas City: Beacon Hill Press, 1948), p. 73.

88. *Ibid.,* p. 75.

89. *Ibid.,* p. 74.

90. *Ibid.*

91. *Ibid.,* p. 75.

White was careful to use this tense with some caution in teaching the instantaneousness of the second blessing, yet he did employ it in this connection.

Charles Ewing Brown, with Hills and Wiley and White, one of the strongest theologians in the Holiness movement's history, was a Church of God (Anderson, Ind.) scholar. In his thorough book *The Meaning of Sanctification,* he devotes a 12-page chapter to the baptism with the Holy Spirit.

Speaking of the various "Pentecosts" in Acts, Brown says, "In every one of these instances there is reasonable evidence that the persons thus baptized with the Holy Ghost were previously converted—were truly regenerated believers."[92] He also viewed Christ's prayer for the sanctification of His disciples as answered at Pentecost.[93]

It is interesting that Brown (in distinction from so many others) is aware that "the early Wesleyan theologians" viewed Pentecost differently. He writes, "Even the early Wesleyan theologians were so far misled . . . that they failed to put proper emphasis on the baptism of the Holy Spirit."[94] He adds, "They tended to interpret sanctification as a crisis experience, it is true, but found most of their texts in other parts of the New Testament."[95] Brown himself says that "the scriptural description of that baptism with the Holy Spirit specifically describes it as a purification of the heart."[96] Here he is thinking especially of Acts 15:8-9.

III. THE HOLINESS MOVEMENT: PRESENT PERIOD

Several factors characterize the Holiness movement's present period. One is that we are enjoying better scholarship. For the most part, the literature is more substantial. Several Ph.D. dissertations have been written on the subject, some of which have been published in book form—works by such persons as George Allen Turner, Leo Cox, and Charles Jones.

---

92. Charles Ewing Brown, *The Meaning of Sanctification* (Anderson, Ind.: The Warner Press, 1945), p. 104.
93. *Ibid.,* p. 109.
94. *Ibid.,* p. 115.
95. *Ibid.*
96. *Ibid.*

With five holiness theological seminaries today, persons designated for holiness ministry become better educated than previously, and this makes both the clergy and laity more demanding of scholarly materials.

The literature is not only more scholarly, but it is far more biblical—even exegetically biblical. Earlier, the Bible was often considered but one of several supports for the doctrine, along with the philosophical, the psychological, etc. But the Holiness movement is freeing itself from an earlier subservience to philosophy for the doctrine's support. Scripture is highly important to us today. Philosophy and psychology have their place, but only as they are ways of understanding the one source—Scripture.

S. S. White, in his *Five Cardinal Elements,* supported each aspect of the doctrine of entire sanctification from three rather equally treated standpoints: Scripture, reason, and experience—which is more or less what John Wesley did. But today, most are interested only in the biblical, and in the other areas only insofar as they throw light on the Bible's meaning. If Scripture clearly teaches something, that is all we need to know. If it suits human reason, fine; if it really does not, too bad for human reason.

tradition

The same goes for psychology, or sociology, or whatever. All these areas serve only to interpret and apply Scripture. They are not sources of authority alongside of Scripture. And they are not even corroborative or confirming of Scripture in the sense that they make any more true or valid what it indeed teaches.

Another trend of the present period is that much of the literature is again being written for the larger Holiness movement and not so much for a given denomination. We are more aware of each other. Many publishing projects are joint endeavors, the various "Aldersgate" programs being typical of this. The Wesleyan Theological Society brings scholars together for the reading of papers, and publishes the *Wesleyan Theological Journal.* The Christian Holiness Association has been revitalized in recent years with well-attended annual conventions.

The current writers on the doctrine of holiness stay close to traditional Holiness movement views, though with some variations.

William M. Greathouse, one of the more prolific writers, locates decidedly on the side of Spirit-baptism entire sanctification. He knows Wesley well, having taught large classes in Wesley's theology for a number of years at Nazarene Theological Seminary while serving as its president. Yet, in distinction from Wesley, his published work is "Holiness movement" on the issue of Spirit baptism.

Greathouse feels that the association of Pentecost with regeneration is a view that does not merit his considering it. He calls it a "strained assumption,"[97] and says, "Birth precedes baptism—in the realm of the flesh and in the realm of the Spirit. Each is complete and distinct within itself. Birth suggests the impartation of life; baptism connotes cleansing."[98] He therefore agrees with Wesley and the Holiness movement generally in understanding that we receive the Spirit in a certain way at conversion. He writes, "That there *is* a reception of the Spirit at justification must not only be admitted but emphasized by those who subscribe to the authority of the New Testament (Gal. 3:1-2). All believers have the Holy Spirit."[99] He goes on to support this from Rom. 8:9 (and 1 Cor. 3:16; 6:19; Eph. 2:2). He continues: "The birth of the Spirit is that act of God by which a soul . . . is made alive to God; the baptism with the Spirit is the bringing of that new life under the full and absolute [a bit strong] control of the Holy Spirit."[100]

Greathouse sees John the Baptist's prophecy of Pentecost (Matt. 3:11-12; Mark 1:8; Luke 3:16-17) as an "allusion to the prophecy of Malachi, particularly to 3:1-6 where we read: 'Who may abide the day of his coming? and who shall stand when he appeareth? for *he is like a refiner's fire,* and like fullers' soap (Mal. 3:2).'" He also sees Pentecost as fulfilling prophecies in Joel, Jeremiah, and Ezekiel. He sees Ezek. 36:25-27 as "the *locus classicus* for the position that the promised gift of the Spirit would mean sanctification and moral enablement."[101]

---

97. William M. Greathouse, *The Fullness of the Spirit* (Kansas City: Beacon Hill Press, 1959), p. 81.

98. *Ibid.*

99. Greathouse, "Full Salvation and Its Concomitants," *The Word and the Doctrine,* ed. Kenneth Geiger (Kansas City: Beacon Hill Press of Kansas City, 1965), p. 217.

100. *Ibid.,* p. 218.

101. *Ibid.,* p. 219.

The most significant matter of all is that Greathouse views Pentecost as the time when believers were cleansed from sin. For example, he says, "Wesleyans believe that Pentecost brings heart purity,"[102] also, "The baptism with the Spirit is a fiery, purifying process which purges the dross of sin from the hearts of its recipients,"[103] and "From our Wesleyan perspective the Pentecostal baptism with the Holy Spirit purges the heart of the believer from sin."[104] Perhaps one more quotation from his pen could be added: "The permanent pattern for all time for Pentecost was purity of heart through the baptism with the Holy Spirit."[105]

While, as has been mentioned earlier, some Wesleyans just now are questioning the repeating of Pentecost in the sense that we today have "Pentecosts," Greathouse affirms its experiential, though not historical, repeatability. He feels that it was repeated for Cornelius and his household, and makes point of the fact that, here, "baptized" is used of what happened. He, with others, quotes Acts 2:39, "The promise is for you and your children, and for all who are far off, as many as the Lord our God shall call to Himself" and affirms that this "far off people" includes ourselves.[106]

William Greathouse locates powerfully with the Holiness movement. If he has known all along that Wesley, whom he esteems so much, viewed the matter differently, he does not

---

102. William Greathouse, "Who Is the Holy Spirit?" *Herald of Holiness,* 61 (May 10, 1972), pp. 8-12. This article is quoted in Charles Carter, *The Person and Ministry of the Holy Spirit* (Grand Rapids: Baker Book House, 1974), p. 158.

103. Greathouse, "Full Salvation and Its Concomitants," p. 220. I do not believe that, by "process" here, he means that it is received gradually, for here, and frequently, he calls it a "baptism."

104. Greathouse, "Who Is the Holy Spirit?" p. 8.

105. Greathouse, *Fullness of the Spirit,* p. 83.

106. Some have used Acts 2:38 to try to show that the baptism with the Holy Spirit is simultaneous with conversion. Peter here says, "Repent, and let each of you be baptized in the name of Jesus Christ for the forgiveness of your sins; and you shall receive the gift of the Holy Spirit" (Acts 2:38). I myself, however, feel that this clearly teaches that the gift of the Holy Spirit will be subsequent to forgiveness, for water baptism will have already taken place.

mention it. He repeatedly calls himself a "Wesleyan."[107]
George A. Turner realizes that Wesley himself does not
associate the Spirit baptism with entire sanctification, yet
aligns himself with the view of the Holiness movement in general that entire sanctification is effected by the Spirit baptism.[108]

About the two baptisms, with water and with the Spirit,
Turner explains:

> The baptism with the Spirit is distinct from baptism
> with water; both are to be perpetuated simultaneously as
> separate baptisms. In the Gospels and Acts the difference
> is made emphatic and explicit (Matt. 3:11; Mark 1:8; Luke
> 3:16; John 1:33; Acts 1:5; 9:18; 11:16; 19:2-6). To make them
> synonymous (baptismal regeneration) is contrary to the
> spirit and letter of the New Testament.[109]

Turner suggests that in the Synoptics and Acts we have
references to the Spirit baptism which are comparable to other
kinds of teachings, such as on faith found in Paul's letters. He
says, "It [the Synoptic—Acts emphasis] has been linked with
the Pauline emphasis on faith to form the idea of a crisis in the
life of the believer, a crisis in which the infilling of the Spirit
coincides with entire sanctification, and issues in purity, power,
and effectiveness."[110] Then he adds, "These three emphases—
faith, baptism, and purification—are found united only in Acts
15:9 (cf. 26:18)."[111] In his recent book, *Christian Holiness,*
Turner says, "The work of the Spirit in *entire* sanctification
is seen in Acts 15:9 where Peter summed up the significance
of Pentecost and also his experience in Cornelius' home by
saying, 'He [God] made no distinction between us and them,
but cleansed their hearts by faith'" (RSV).[112]

In more overarching teachings Turner says, "Pentecost is

---

107. It is not insignificant that in a recent unpublished paper on the subject, Greathouse takes what he understands to be a holistic view of the baptism
with the Holy Spirit. While he feels he is stressing that entire sanctification is
accomplished by the baptism, he argues what he considers to be a more inclusive view in harmony with his understanding of Wesley's thought.

108. Turner, *Vision Which Transforms,* pp. 149 ff.

109. *Ibid.,* p. 152.

110. Turner, *More Excellent Way,* pp. 106 ff.

111. *Ibid.*

112. George A. Turner, *Christian Holiness* (Kansas City: Beacon Hill
Press of Kansas City, 1977), p. 74.

not presented as initiation into discipleship; rather it brings purifying (Acts 15:9) and empowering (Acts 1:8) to those already discipled or converted."[113] He argues for the need for the disciples, who were Christians, to be cleansed, when he says:

> In spite of the fact that their names were written in heaven and hence we would call them *converted* prior to Pentecost, still they had many evidences of "the old nature." They showed worldly attitudes such as intolerance, pride, selfishness, race prejudices, and fear. To all of these they present marked contrasts after Pentecost.[114]

One of the most prolific of present-day holiness writers, W. T. Purkiser, says: "In a word, the baptism and consequent fullness of the Spirit are the means by which entire sanctification is wrought."[115] He is particularly strong in opposing the view of gradual sanctification. He says, "A baptism with the Holy Spirit as with fire could no more be a gradual, never-completed process than could a baptism with water. Both, in the very nature of the case, must be acts which take place at a given time."[116]

Notwithstanding the fact that Wesley did not associate entire sanctification with Pentecost, Purkiser writes, "It is our conviction that the New Testament gives abundant warrant for assuming that the baptism with the Spirit and entire sanctification are two aspects of one and the same work of divine grace in Christian hearts."[117]

His more recent book, *Interpreting Christian Holiness,* sums up his basic position. For example, he views Christ's prayer for sanctification as answered at Pentecost. He says:

> The Book of Acts records the fulfillment of the promise and prayer of Jesus concerning the Holy Spirit. While the Jerusalem Pentecost of Acts 2 had an unrepeatable, historical side to it as the beginning of the long-awaited "age of the Spirit," its deeper personal meaning is attested by the

---

113. *Ibid.,* p. 73.
114. *Ibid.,* p. 74.
115. W. T. Purkiser, *Sanctification and Its Synonyms* (Kansas City: Beacon Hill Press of Kansas City, 1961), p. 25.
116. *Ibid.,* pp. 28-29.
117. W. T. Purkiser, *Conflicting Concepts of Holiness* (Kansas City: Beacon Hill Press, 1953), p. 64.

Samaritan Pentecost of Acts 8, the Caesarean or Gentile Pentecost of Acts 10, and the Ephesian Pentecost of Acts 19.[118]

Richard S. Taylor has long taken this kind of view. In his "Doctrine of Holiness" section of the recent symposium, *God, Man, and Salvation,* he treats it with some thoroughness. In a summarizing way he says, "There is adequate basis in the New Testament for linking together entire sanctification and the baptism with the Holy Spirit. This baptism is distinct from and subsequent to the birth of the Spirit."[119] Similarly he holds to such basic positions as that the disciples were Christian believers prior to Pentecost, that holiness "is perfected in the baptism with the Holy Spirit,"[120] and that Jesus' prayer, "Sanctify them" (John 17:17), "obviously found its fulfillment on the Day of Pentecost."[121] In a capsulizing statement, he says, "When men are sanctified wholly they are baptized with the Holy Spirit, and when they are baptized with the Holy Spirit they are sanctified wholly."[122]

Numerous other more recent Holiness movement authors have likewise taught that entire sanctification is wrought by the baptism with the Holy Spirit. These include the late D. Shelby Corlett (who wrote extensively on the subject), the late J. Glenn Gould, Donald Metz, Willard H. Taylor, and Arnold E. Airhart.[123] Indeed, before the 1970s perhaps not a single

---

118. W. T. Purkiser, *Interpreting Christian Holiness* (Kansas City: Beacon Hill Press of Kansas City, 1971), p. 14.

119. Richard S. Taylor, doctrine of holiness treatment in *God, Man, and Salvation,* W. T. Purkiser, Richard S. Taylor, and Willard H. Taylor (Kansas City: Beacon Hill Press of Kansas City, 1977), p. 506.

120. Richard S. Taylor, *Preaching Holiness Today* (Kansas City: Beacon Hill Press of Kansas City, 1968), p. 46.

121. Richard S. Taylor, *Life in the Spirit* (Kansas City: Beacon Hill Press of Kansas City, 1966), p. 82.

122. *Ibid.*

123. D. Shelby Corlett, *The Baptism with the Holy Spirit* (Kansas City: Beacon Hill Press, n.d.); *Lord of All* (Kansas City: Beacon Hill Press of Kansas City, 1964); *God in the Present Tense; the Person and Work of the Holy Spirit* (Kansas City: Beacon Hill Press of Kansas City, 1974); J. Glenn Gould, *The Whole Counsel of God* (Kansas City: Beacon Hill Press, 1945), p. 104; Donald Metz, *Studies in Biblical Holiness,* p. 111; Willard H. Taylor, "The Baptism with the Holy Spirit: Promise of Grace or Judgment?" *Wesleyan Theological Journal,* 12 (Spring, 1977), pp. 16-25; and Arnold E. Airhart, *Acts,* "Beacon Bible Expositions," vol. V, ed. William Greathouse and Willard Taylor (Kansas City: Beacon Hill Press of Kansas City, 1977), p. 124.

book was authored by a holiness scholar in the previous 100 years or so, that had not taken the position that Pentecost was the time of the entire sanctification of the 120 disciples.

Since entire sanctification is wrought by a baptism, the baptism with the Holy Spirit, this also augurs for its instantaneousness, to which subject we now turn.

Chapter 6

Instantaneous Versus Gradual Sanctification

Both John Wesley and the Holiness movement writers taught, and the present holiness writers teach, that entire sanctification is instantaneous. But Wesley himself also taught gradual sanctification, by which he seems to have meant a gradual "mortification" of original sin. Several Holiness movement writers have used gradual and progressive sanctification terms, of their views; but they have meant by the terms, not a gradual cleansing away of original sin, but growth in grace, a gradual preparation of the mind and heart for the all-at-once cleansing. Others have studiedly avoided such terms, and have made it obviously clear that they did not teach that original sin is cleansed away gradually. This has been the usual approach in the Holiness movement.

I. Bases for the Instantaneous Emphasis

A number of bases have been given, in holiness literature, for the teaching that entire sanctification is received instantaneously.

A. Because It Is by a Baptism

As has already been discussed, the 120 disciples in the Upper Room were already believers, and on the Day of Pentecost they received entire sanctification. At that time, Jesus' prayer, "Sanctify them" (John 17:17), was answered. Since the

A one time event

An action of complete follow-through

disciples, thus prayed for, were already sanctified in the sense of being set apart for God's use (because they already had been chosen and ordained), the sanctification Christ prayed for was sanctification in the sense of being made pure through the cleansing away of original sin.

It was a cleansing because it was a baptism, for that is one of the meanings of baptism. It was a cleansing, also, because it was described as a purification of their hearts in Acts 15:9; also, because it was "with fire"—the burning up of chaff, and a purging. All these are aspects of the cleansing that was to obtain when Jesus would baptize with the Holy Spirit according to Matt. 3:11-12.

The Spirit baptism, then, is the time when a believer is cleansed from original sin; and this cleansing, this sanctification, is instantaneous, in part, because it is effected by a baptism. Baptism is by its very nature punctiliar: it happens at one time, at a given time. A person is not partially baptized, and later fully baptized. Nor is one gradually baptized. It is not a matter of more-or-less, or of degrees. One is baptized, period.

Even as regeneration is not gradual, so the second work of grace is not received gradually. True, there is gradual preparation of the mind and heart for the fiery Spirit baptism which effects entire sanctification, but there is no gradual purification. Original sin is cleansed, expelled, eradicated, destroyed, at one stroke, by this Spirit baptism. It is not cleansed gradually, piecemeal, one aspect of it after another.

Since, as we saw in an earlier chapter, Wesley did not teach that entire sanctification is received by a "Spirit baptism," it is somewhat understandable why he would teach a kind of gradualism concerning entire sanctification—as well as its instantaneousness. In illustrating his thought on gradual sanctification, Wesley said that it is received in the way that a gradual physical death occurs.

It should be noted that physical death is a useable analogy, since, in Romans 6, death is used by Paul as analogous to what happens to original sin. But there are various ways to die. Since Paul used aorist-tense verbs for such, he was perhaps writing of a different type of death than Wesley was. He was possibly referring to the kind that happens in a punctiliar way, as in a heart attack or an accident; not the kind that happens after a slow ebbing of life as is often the case in cancer deaths.

B. *Because It Is a Sealing*

As earlier stated, three times in the New Testament (2 Cor. 1:22; Eph. 1:13; 4:30) the figure of "sealing" seems to be a symbol of entire sanctification. It is one of the several concomitants of entire sanctification, suggesting God's ownership of us and His approval of our lives. Like baptism, it suggests instantaneousness. A person did not keep on, more and more, sealing a letter with hot wax to assure that the person whose it was would be the one permitted to open it.

In 2 Cor. 1:22 Paul says, "He who establishes us with you in Christ and anointed us is God, who also sealed us and gave *us* the Spirit in our hearts as a pledge." While Paul does not refer here, or anywhere, to the baptism with the Holy Spirit, in specific terms, the implication is strong that this sealing occurred when believers received the baptism with the Spirit. This sealing is connected with being established, which is one of the results of entire sanctification (see 1 Thess. 3:10, 13; 5:23). He establishes us by giving us the Spirit, having sealed us— once again an aorist participle *(sphragisamenos)*.

Something similar is found in Eph. 1:13, where Paul writes, "In Him, you also, after listening to the message of truth, the gospel of your salvation—having also believed, you were sealed in Him with the Spirit of promise." After "listening," and "having also believed" (become justified), they were "sealed." This sealing is clearly subsequent to believing, and it is a sealing in which God more fully approves us and more truly "owns" us. Note also that they were sealed "with the Holy Spirit of promise" (the Spirit which had been promised). He was promised in Joel 2:28 where we read, "I will pour out My Spirit on all mankind" (fulfilled on the Day of Pentecost, Acts 2:16). The Spirit was promised by John the Baptist who said, "He Himself will baptize you with the Holy Spirit and fire" (Matt. 3:11). He was promised by Jesus himself in Acts 1:5 where, just before the Ascension, He said, "John baptized with water, but you shall be baptized with the Holy Spirit not many days from now."

The other reference to sealing is Eph. 4:30 which reads, "Do not grieve the Holy Spirit of God, by whom you were sealed for the day of redemption"; but this particular reference does not add anything to what the other two passages teach.

Sealing, then, is subsequent to justification, and is received when the Holy Spirit is given in a special way, and symbolizes instantaneousness.[1]

C. Because It Is a Circumcision

In Colossians, Paul uses circumcision as analogous to entire sanctification. He says, "In Him you were also circumcised with a circumcision made without hands, in the removal of the body of the flesh by the circumcision of Christ" (2:11). This NASB rendering is quite different from the KJV reading which introduces three words that are not in the Greek and thus distort what Paul is saying. The KJV reads, "In whom also ye are circumcised . . . without hands, in putting off the body of the sins of the flesh." The "sins of the flesh" would mean a whole group of sin acts. But "of the sins" is not in the Greek, and what Paul is saying is that the "body of the flesh" is circumcised. That is, the state or condition or principle of the flesh is circumcised or cut away as in the Jewish ritual of circumcision.

As with baptism, so with circumcision: it is not a more-and-more matter. One is not gradually circumcised. A person is not a little more circumcised one day than he was the previous day. It is something accomplished instantaneously, in a moment, in an act—in a decisive act.

Besides the figures of baptism, sealing, and circumcision, other symbols of the second blessing which suggest its instantaneousness include the "filled" (of Acts 2:4, etc., but not of Eph. 5:18, where the present tense appears), "anointed" (2 Cor. 1:21), "pour forth" (Acts 2:17), "poured forth" (Acts 2:33), "fell" (Acts 10:44), and "poured out" (Acts 10:45). None of these is done in a continuous way.

D. Because It Is Received by Faith

Another significant basis for the view, in both Wesley and the Holiness movement, that entire sanctification is instantaneous is because it is received, not by works, but by faith. If it were by works, then it would be gradual, and gradual only.

---

1. See a good discussion of sealing, including what I have not discussed, the "pledge" or "earnest," in Mahan's *Baptism of the Holy Ghost*, pp. 23-24.

If by works, it would be a more-and-more matter, and would never be complete or fully obtained.

This was a cardinal teaching of Wesley who maintained that even as we are justified by faith alone, we are sanctified wholly by faith alone. Luther had taught, of course, that we are justified by faith alone, but that we are sanctified gradually by pious disciplines—as is taught in Calvinistic theology as well. This caused Wesley to say that hardly anyone had taught better than Luther had on justification; nor more poorly than Luther had on sanctification.

Wesley and the Holiness movement, in teaching that entire sanctification is received by faith, teach what the New Testament itself does. In Acts 15:8-9, Peter says, "God . . . made no distinction between us [at Pentecost] and them [Cornelius and his household], cleansing their hearts by faith." Further, in Luke's reporting of Paul's testimony about his call to preach, in Acts 26:18, Paul says he was designated for a Gentile ministry, "that they may receive forgiveness of sins and an inheritance among those who have been sanctified by faith in Me [Christ]."

The faith which procures entire sanctification might, nevertheless, have about it a durative quality. A believer might exercise for some time an expectant trust that God will sanctify him wholly before his entire sanctification occurs. Even so, the actual experience is instantaneous. If this grace were gradual, then it might be received by works of piety. But works is not the way into this grace; faith is the route one takes. And while faith might have about it an extended quality, faith as the means of obtainment suggests that any consecrated believer may, at any instant, exercise the believing trust which results in God's grace of entire sanctification.

E. *Because of the Aorist Tense*

The aorist tense, in the Greek New Testament, in which the verbal cognates of *hagiadzo*, for "sanctify," are often found, also suggests the instantaneousness of sanctification. This word, in its verbal forms, appears 28 times in the New Testament. It is in the aorist tense 12 times, in the perfect tense 7 times, and in the present tense 9 times. The aorist tense, the most common one in the Greek, appears also in numerous other words that relate to entire sanctification, besides "sanctify," such as in "supply" (1 Thess. 3:10) and "establish" (1 Thess. 3:13) and "present" (Rom. 12:1).

Some difference of view exists even among holiness writers, on the significance of the aorist tense as supportive of entire sanctification doctrine. Yet Greek experts such as A. T. Robertson, H. V. P. Nunn, Daniel Steele,[2] and others, explain the meaning of the aorist tense in such a way that its New Testament usage is significant as confirming the crisic and the completed character of the second work of grace.

The evidence is sufficient for H. Orton Wiley to say that the aorist tense "denotes a momentary, completed act without reference to time,"[3] and for W. T. Purkiser to call the use of this tense an "impressive line of evidence for the instantaneousness of sanctification."[4] While Wiley and Purkiser are theologians, and not Greek experts as such, long-time Greek professor Richard Howard says that "the basic significance of the aorist . . . is that it depicts a *crisis act* in distinction from a *progressive process.*"[5]

This tense denotes punctiliar, momentary, decisive action, and sometimes completed action, whatever the mood which accompanies the tense. If the mood is indicative, it denotes crisic or completed action that has already happened. If the mood is vocative, as in 1 Thess. 5:23, we have a wish or a prayer that a decisive, momentary sanctification will occur. If the Greek is speaking of something that will happen repeatedly, the imperfect tense will likely be used; if continuously, the present tense. If a past, decisive action is denoted, the results of which continue into the present, the perfect tense will likely be found. (This perfect tense, actually, along with the aorist tense, is also indicative of the crisic character of entire sanctification, as it appears in various "holiness" passages.)

It is a fact that, besides the punctiliar action denoted by

2. See A. T. Robertson, *A Grammar of the Greek New Testament in the Light of Historical Research* (Nashville: The Broadman Press, 1914); H. V. P. Nunn, *A Short Syntax of New Testament Greek* (Cambridge: The University Press, 1924); William W. Goodwin, *A Greek Grammar* (Boston: Grinnand Co., 1892); Daniel Steele, *Milestone Papers* (New York: Nelson and Phillips, 1878).

3. Wiley, *Christian Theology*, 2:447.

4. Purkiser, *Conflicting Concepts of Holiness*, p. 34.

5. Richard Howard, *Newness of Life* (Kansas City: Beacon Hill Press of Kansas City, 1975), p. 170.

the aorist tense, it sometimes denotes what is not altogether dissimilar: completed action. An example of completed action is where an aorist is used for the building of the temple, when the specific passage states that it took "forty-six years" (John 2:20). Often, however, the aorist word itself or the wider context, where an aorist is used, shows that crisic, as well as completed action, is what is denoted. For example, when "sealing" is in the aorist tense it would denote a given completed action that would take only a moment to accomplish. Thus it would signify momentary or crisic action.

In any case, whether crisic or completed action is denoted, the aorist tense would support the holiness emphasis upon a grace which has already been obtained or is to be obtained. It would undermine a sanctification that is gradually received all through one's life. While "kind of action," and not the time involved, is the significant matter in the Greek tenses, the kind of action denoted by the aorist tense suggests, not the gradual, but the instantaneous and the completed crucifixion of the Adamic, fleshly nature. As A. T. Robinson says, "The three kinds of action [aorist, present, and perfect] are thus momentary or punctiliar when action is regarded as a whole and may be represented by a dot (.), linear or durative action which may be represented by a continuous line (___), the continuance of perfected or completed action which may be represented by this graph (.___)."[6]

II. WESLEY AND CLARKE CONTRASTED

John Wesley taught that prior to entire sanctification there is a gradual sanctification which is preparatory. By this gradual sanctification he sometimes seemed to mean a gradual lessening of original sin. He spoke of "a gradual mortification of sin."[7] In the same work, *A Plain Account,* which he revised rather late in his life, and so reflected there his mature thought, he suggests that entire sanctification is analogous to a slow, physical death. He says, "A man may be dying for some time; yet he does not,

---

6. A. T. Robertson, *A Grammar of the New Testament in the Light of Historical Research* (New York: George H. Doran Co., 1949), p. 825.
7. Wesley, *Plain Account,* p. 61.

properly speaking, die, till the soul is separated from the body. . . . In like manner, he may be dying to sin for some time; yet he is not dead to sin till sin is separated from his soul."[8]

A bit farther on in *A Plain Account,* Wesley speaks of "a gradual work of God in the soul," and of "many years, before sin is destroyed," but adds, "It need not, therefore, be affirmed over and over . . . that there is a gradual work of God in the soul, or that, generally speaking, it is a long time, even many years, before sin is destroyed."[9]

In answer to the question whether faith is the condition or the instrument of sanctification he says, "It is both the condition and instrument of it. When we begin to believe, then sanctification begins. And as faith increases, holiness increases, till we are created new."[10] If sanctification can "begin," and if it can increase as faith increases, we seem to be talking about a process of gradual sanctification. Wynkoop thinks so, for, of this, in Wesley, she says, "In this passage the process aspect of sanctification is clearly indicated."[11]

It is well to note the fact, however, that Wesley wrote to his brother Charles urging him to "press the *instantaneous* blessing," adding, "then I shall have more time for my peculiar calling, enforcing the *gradual* work."[12]

Wesley's younger contemporary, Adam Clarke, taught differently. While Clarke sometimes dissociates Pentecost from entire sanctification in his *Commentary,* he nonetheless believes that we are not sanctified wholly in a gradual way. "In no part of the Scriptures," he says, "are we directed to seek holiness *gradatim.* We are to come to God as well for an instantaneous and complete purification from all sin as for an instantaneous pardon. Neither the *gradatim pardon* nor the seriatim purification exists in the Bible."[13] Clarke would evidently admit that much growth in grace can be expected

---

8. *Ibid.,* p. 62.
9. *Ibid.,* p. 90.
10. Wesley, *Works,* 8:279.
11. Mildred Bangs Wynkoop, *A Theology of Love* (Kansas City: Beacon Hill Press of Kansas City, 1972), p. 109.
12. Wesley, *Letters,* 5:16.
13. Adam Clarke, *Entire Sanctification* (Louisville: Pentecostal Publishing Co., n.d.), p. 38.

after entire sanctification, but he would not call this gradual sanctification. His next words are, "It is when the soul is purified from all sin that it can properly grow in grace, and in the knowledge of our Lord Jesus Christ."[14]

III. The Holiness Movement Position

On this issue of gradual sanctification, the Holiness movement preferred Clarke's view to that of Wesley. For example, J. A. Wood, a Methodist, taught, with Clarke, only instantaneous sanctification—not the gradual. In the 1861 edition of his *Perfect Love* he writes, "The beautiful analogy in the conditions and experience of regeneration and entire sanctification, favors the idea of an *instantaneous* sanctification similar to regeneration."[15] Since they are both received by faith, an instantaneousness applies to entire sanctification as obviously as to regeneration.

Wood illustrates by saying that even as "the soul does not leave the body by *parts,* "[16] so original sin does not become expelled in parts. Wood also says, "He who seeks the gradual attainment of entire sanctification seeks necessarily something *less* than entire sanctification *now;* that is, he does not seek entire sanctification at all."[17] Wood continues, "The faith which is the proximate condition of entire sanctification can only be exercised in connection with the *renunciation of all sin,* and *complete submission to God.* "[18] He underscores the instantaneousness further with these words: "Grace . . . is not implanted in the soul gradually; neither is inbred sin, the antagonism to grace, exterminated from the soul gradually."[19]

Relating growth to the process prior to regeneration he says, "The sinner undergoes a similar process before his conversion; but his receiving *light* and *conviction,* and his con-

---

14. *Ibid.*
15. J. A. Wood, *Perfect Love,* 1861 edition (Philadelphia: S. D. Burlock), p. 75.
16. *Ibid.,* p. 76.
17. *Ibid.,* p. 55.
18. *Ibid.*
19. *Ibid.,* pp. 63-64.

fessions, prayers, and *repentance,* do not *convert* him. They only precede his conversion."[20]

Some 20 years later, in his revision of *Perfect Love,* Wood is at least as vigorous, if not more so, in his opposition to gradual sanctification. He is confident that it does not accord with our experience. He writes:

> The uniform experience of all who are clear in the light of personal holiness teaches that purification is instantaneous *and not gradual.* Experience has but one voice on this subject, i.e., that it was sought by consecration and faith, and received the same as regeneration, by direct divine power. *Gradualism* does not accord with the experience of those who profess perfect love. The instantaneous does.[21]

As much respected for scholarship, perhaps, as any Holiness movement writer, and writing about as voluminously, was Daniel Steele. He strongly supported the instantaneousness of entire sanctification. He writes:

> When we come to consider the *work of purification* in the believer's soul, by the power of the Holy Spirit, both in the new birth and in entire sanctification, we find that *the aorist is almost uniformly used.* This tense, according to the best New Testament grammarians, never indicates a continuous, habitual, or repeated act, but one which is momentary, and done once and for all.[22]

Beverly Carradine spoke to the issue of instantaneousness and growth as follows:

> That there is a growth in grace before the reception of this blessing and a rapid growth afterwards, is hereby affirmed, and no intelligent teacher of holiness thinks of denying. But neither the ante growth or the post growth is the work itself of which we speak. That work, which cleanses the heart from *all* sin, no matter how preceded by mortification of spirit and crucifying of the flesh, is done in a moment, in the twinkling of an eye, by the mighty power of God.[23]

Early 20-century holiness evangelist C. W. Ruth preached that we are not made a little holy, then more and most holy,

---

20. *Ibid.,* p. 59.
21. *Ibid.,* p. 92.
22. Daniel Steele, *Mile-Stone Papers* (New York: Eaton and Mains, 1878), pp. 65-66.
23. Carradine, *Sanctified Life,* p. 17.

and that therefore there is no gradual purification.[24] E. F. Walker was likewise clear in the matter of growth versus instantaneousness. He says, "Any religious system which teaches that we are sanctified by development, good works, suffering, or in any other way than by grace through faith, may be Pelagianism, Unitarianism, or Romanism; but the gospel of Christ it certainly is not."[25] Walker exegetes Jesus' prayer, "Sanctify them," as further support for his teaching that entire sanctification is instantaneous and not gradual. He writes:

> If that prayer was ever answered, and we believe it was answered on the Day of Pentecost, the disciples were at once made holy. They could grow in grace before and after their sanctification, and no doubt they did. But suddenly, in the Upper Room, the sanctifying Spirit accomplished this work in them. And this is still the law of the Spirit of life in Christ Jesus: growth in holiness, but instant sanctification.[26]

In Britain at century's turn Thomas Cook was also teaching against gradual purification, and using arguments and analogies similar to those being used in the American Holiness movement. He says that "holiness is both a *crisis* and a *process,*"[27] and quotes Bishop Moule as saying, "'It is a crisis with a view to a process.'"[28] He notes the distinction between "purity" and "growth," pointing out that the one is negative and the other positive. And he explains, "Purity and growth are as distinct in their offices as the work of two men on a building—one is removing the rubbish, the other is enlarging

---

24. Ruth, *Entire Sanctification,* pp. 17-18. Ruth says: "In this connection it is well to note that this human side of sanctification,—which is but the approach to, and the condition of *entire* sanctification—may be gradual. That is, the individual may be some time in entirely completing this 'separation', 'dedication' and 'devotement' of his all to God. But the moment this human side of sanctification is completed, and every condition met, faith in reality touching the promise, the divine side of sanctification, which is 'to make holy or pure; to make free from sin, to cleanse from moral corruption and pollution, to purify,' is instantaneously and divinely inwrought by the application of the virtue of the atonement through the power of the Holy Ghost. In the language of Adam Clarke: 'Neither the *gradatim* pardon nor the *seriatim* purification exists in the Bible'" (*ibid.,* pp. 16-17).
25. Walker, *Sanctify Them,* pp. 58-59.
26. *Ibid.,* p. 55.
27. Thomas Cook, *New Testament Holiness* (London: The Epworth Press, 1950), p. 43.
28. *Ibid.*

and beautifying the structure."[29] They are different also because our part in each of them is of a different kind. He says, "In growth we are active and cooperative, but in entire cleansing the soul is passive; it is something experienced, the same as regeneration."[30]

Even as there are no degrees in regeneration, there are none, for Cook, in entire sanctification. He writes, "There are no degrees of pardon: it is full, perfect, and complete."[31] He continues, "In like manner, while the negative aspect of holiness is the purging of the heart from all that is carnal—and this is a full, complete and entire work, without degrees and gradualism—there is also a positive aspect of holiness."[32] The phrase "without degrees and gradualism" is particularly significant.[33]

In both his books on holiness doctrine, S. S. White emphasized the instantaneousness of entire sanctification and opposed gradual sanctification. In *Eradication,* in which he supported even the use of this term as well as what it means, he writes, "Entire sanctification results in an integration of personality [which may be questioned] which comes, not by growth or development, but rather by the eradication of the contrary principle of sin, with which every part of Adam's fallen race is afflicted."[34]

While Wiley did not write any separate book on entire sanctification, he treats it with considerable thoroughness in his three-volume *Christian Theology.* He understands that we receive initial sanctification at conversion. He writes, "Regeneration . . . is the impartation of a life that is holy in its nature; and concomitant with it, is an initial holiness or cleansing from guilt and acquired depravity."[35] Besides this initial sanctification, a believer may receive entire sanctification. But for Wiley,

---

29. *Ibid.,* p. 42.
30. *Ibid.*
31. *Ibid.*
32. *Ibid.,* p. 46.
33. Some things Cook says do not locate him necessarily in opposition to gradual sanctification. For an example, he writes, "We do not mean instantaneous in the same sense as a flash of lightning, or an explosion of gunpowder, but in the sense in which death is instantaneous. 'A man may be a long time dying, but there is a moment when he dies'" (*Ibid.,* p. 40).
34. White, *Eradication,* p. 74.
35. Wiley, *Christian Theology,* 2:446.

there is no gradual sanctification. He says, "Now this holiness already begun [in initial sanctification] is to be perfected by the cleansing at a single stroke of inbred sin."[36]

Richard Taylor speaks of "progressive sanctification."[37] But this is only "the progressive establishment of one's Christian character."[38] He makes it clear that progressive sanctification is "not an increase of . . . essential holiness as far as purity . . . is concerned."[39] Elsewhere, speaking of the fact that Christians are to "grow in grace" (2 Pet. 3:18), he says, "This is intended to be a growth within holiness, not growth toward its attainment."[40] He continues by saying, "Jesus, too, as a boy 'increased in wisdom and in stature, and in favor [*charis,* grace] with God and man' (Luke 2:52); but this can hardly be construed as an improvement in His holiness."[41]

Taylor makes it clear that we do not grow into holiness. Of the view that "growth in holiness constitutes a corresponding decrease in unholiness," he says that it "is tantamount to growing *into* holiness."[42] He himself understands that "holiness is linked to maturity only as its necessary prerequisite."[43] He explains that there is "a growth *in* holiness without such growth constituting a growth *of* holiness."[44] About the "jealousy and strife" at Corinth, he says, "The fault is not legitimate immaturity but carnality, manifested in jealousy and strife."[45] And carnality "requires cleansing to remedy, not the temporal process of growth."[46] He says further, "In one sense only can we properly speak of developing in holiness. This relates to one's growth in love, when love is viewed as an element of holiness."[47]

W. T. Purkiser also sees the matter in this way. He says, "This puts the issue squarely before us. Entire sanctification,

---

36. *Ibid.*
37. Taylor, *Preaching Holiness Today,* p. 55.
38. *Ibid.*
39. *Ibid.*
40. Taylor, *God, Man, and Salvation,* p. 471.
41. *Ibid.*
42. *Ibid.*
43. *Ibid.,* p. 470.
44. *Ibid.*
45. *Ibid.,* p. 471, fn.
46. *Ibid.* (See also Wiley, *Christian Theology,* 2:507.)
47. *Ibid.,* p. 472.

as understood by the holiness people, does not admit of degrees."[48] He continues, "It is as perfect and complete in its kind as the work of regeneration and justification is perfect and complete in its kind."[49] "This does not mean," he explains, "that there is no growth in grace both before and after sanctification. What it does mean is that sanctification, as an act of God, is instantaneous, and is not produced by growth or self-discipline or the progressive control of the carnal nature."[50]

These, then, are biblical and historical supports which, when taken as a whole, throw considerable weight toward the view that entire sanctification is received instantaneously and that, while there is a growth in grace as well as continual cleansing after entire sanctification (1 John 1:7), no gradual cleansing from original sin occurs.

---

48. Purkiser, *Conflicting Concepts,* pp. 30-31.
49. *Ibid.*
50. *Ibid.*

Chapter 7

Carnality and Humanity

Once in this experience of entire sanctification, a person is anxious to exemplify, day by day, the kind of Christian life which is consistent with such a state of grace. But what is to be expected of us . . . by others . . . by ourselves . . . by God? We are still human and subject to errors of judgment, emotional pressures, and prejudices, so that our performance is less than ideal. So the question of what kind of attitude or act is prompted by the carnal nature, and what kind is only human, is of considerable importance.

What are we cleansed from and *not* cleansed from when we are sanctified wholly? What about our essential human nature such as temperament, and aberrated human nature such as acquired prejudices and hostilities? Actions and attitudes might stem from these sources, after a believer has had carnality cleansed from his nature. They would often not be excusable. Yet, if from the human nature, they would not mean that the person is not sanctified wholly. He would therefore have the assurance that he is still in the second grace, and would seek by God's help to correct the aberrant behavior.

A. Constituents of Carnality

Carnality is not necessarily evidenced by a hostility, or an anger, or nervousness, in which a person might become red-necked or lose his emotional equilibrium. Such reaction might stem not from an Adamic detriment, but from natural temperament. It might stem from righteous anger, as was the case with Jesus when He cleansed the Temple; or when He healed a person on the sabbath, and when questioned about it, "looked around at them with anger" (Mark 3:5, RSV). It might arise from resentment toward a parent or a fellow church member due to traumatic experiences in one's early life. It might arise from nervous stress due to physical or emotional problems.

But this is not to depreciate the powerful change in a person's life when he is sanctified wholly. To be cleansed from original sin is a great deal to be cleansed from, actually. Wesley may have overstated it, feeling as he did that the change at our entire sanctification is "immensely greater than that wrought when he [anyone] was justified."[1] Yet, although to be cleansed from carnality is of such great significance, it does not include cleansing from what is essentially human, such as temperament, the sex drive, and the hundred-and-one deficiencies that we come by during this life, such as in the area of racial or economic or educational or geographical prejudices.

Carnality does not in itself bring condemnation. No guilt attaches to it. Thus no one will ever go into perdition for Adam's sin alone. It is true that "all sinned" when Adam sinned, according to Rom. 5:12, where the aorist *hemarton* appears. However, this does not mean "all have sinned" as in the KJV, but "all sinned." We really did sin when our representative did, even as a college really does lose a race when its representative loses. But because of an unconditional benefit of the Atonement—the "free gift" referred to in Rom. 5:15-17 which was given to all— the guilt of Adam's sin has been waived, although the depravity itself, the bias to sin, is cleansed only when believers are baptised with the Holy Spirit.

In support of this view, H. Orton Wiley says, "Thus the condemnation which rested upon the race through Adam's sin is removed by the one oblation of Christ. By this we understand that no child of Adam is condemned eternally, either for the original offense or its consequences. Thus . . . culpability does not attach to original sin."[2] John Wesley was of the same opinion.

---

1. John Wesley, *Plain Account*, p. 61. I question Wesley at this point because to be justified changes our eternal destiny, because at this time we pass from death to life, and because we are then made children of God by adoption. Even the power over us of inbred sin is broken at justification, i.e., the enslavement to inbred sin. In entire sanctification original sin is itself extirpated.

2. Wiley, *Christian Theology*, 2:135.

The imperative to receive this cleansing from carnality is that one will then be in the establishing grace (1 Thess. 3:13) and will not find himself leaning away from God due to the carnal propensity to sin. He will also experience the countless benefits of the Holy Spirit's pervasive indwelling presence to live with a lean toward God.

Carnality is being discussed here principally as the sin which remains in the believer after justification—the state or condition of sin (not an entity, not a thing), which inclines the believer to acts of sin (but does not cause them). It is not to be thought of as a physical substance, but as a state which is relational in which we become estranged from God and biased toward acts of sin. When this exists in the unbeliever, its strength is greater than when in the believer, because it is not then countered by the Holy Spirit (who, as we have already noted, indwells a person after he becomes a believer according to Rom. 8:9 and Gal. 5:17).

Although the word "carnality" might suggest that it relates only to the body, our life in the physical flesh, it includes the entire detriment we have received from the racial fall in Adam. This is why Paul called the Corinthian Christians, "babes in Christ" (1 Cor. 3:3), "yet carnal." They were filled with envy and strife, and were divided into factions.

While the word for "carnal" is a cognate of *sarx,* and while *sarx* has many meanings, including the body and the soft material on the bones of the body, it is often used, particularly by Paul, in an ethical sense, as the opposite of being in the Spirit. Thus we read in Kittel, "For Paul, orientation to the σαρξ *[sarx]* or the πνευμα *[pneuma]*[3] is the total attitude which determines everything. . . . Life is determined as a totality by σαρξ *[sarx]* or πνευμα *[pneuma].*" It is implied that those who are "in the flesh" cannot please God (Rom. 8:8), but that those who are "in the Spirit" (Rom. 8:9) can. One might live "according to the flesh" (Rom. 8:13). However, one might, instead, "belong to Christ" truly because of having "crucified the flesh" (Gal. 5:24).

John Wesley referred to carnality by many terms. He called

3. Edward Schweizer, *Theological Dictionary of the New Testament,* ed. Gerhard Friedrich Kittel, trans. Geoffrey W. Bromiley (Grand Rapids: Wm. B. Eerdmans, 1971), 7:135.

it "pride, self-will, unbelief."[4] Particularly as it indwells believers, he called it a "bent to backsliding," "sin in a believer," "a proneness to depart from God."[5]

It is a total corruption of our nature—a total depravity, arising from being deprived through Adam's fall of certain ministries of the Holy Spirit.[6] Some teach that only the moral nature of man suffered due to the Fall and not his rational nature or his physical nature. And some believe that even the moral nature is not fallen to the extent that no good decisions are possible apart from grace. But this is Pelagian thinking.

A. M. Hills tended toward this concept. He taught that fallen man can implement even a motive to a good action apart from grace. He writes, "We can set aside unworthy motives, and cease thinking of unworthy things; we can enthrone the rational and the moral in our lives, over the incitements of appetite and passion, and thus escape the doom of being the passive victim of impulses to evil."[7] With no mention of grace in this connection, he says that we are "truly the author of our character."[8] Similarly, he says, "We must have this capacity for moral and religious motives, or we are only animals,"[9] and adds, "This conviction of a self-determining power, or a control of the will belonging to us, is as universal as man."[10]

But what of Romans 7, in which Paul says the unregenerate are enslaved to sin so that the good they would do they cannot do and the evil they would not do they do (v. 15)? Jesus said, "For apart from me you can do nothing" (John 15:5). He told us that "a rotten tree [cannot] bring forth good fruit" (Matt. 7:19), and made it clear that of himself man is corrupt when he asked, "How can you, being evil, speak what is good?"

---

4. John Wesley, "On Sin in Believers," *Four Sermons by Wesley* (London: Wesleyan Methodist Book-room, n.d.), p. 13.

5. *Ibid.*

6. The believer has the Holy Spirit indwelling him according to Gal. 5:17, along with the *sarx*, but the unbeliever, apart from prevenient grace, is, due to carnality, dead to God. Original sin is not even partly cleansed at regeneration, and yet its effects in a believer are not as great as in the unbeliever.

7. A. M. Hills, *Fundamental Christian Theology* (Pasadena, Calif.: C. J. Kinne, 1931), 1:362.

8. *Ibid.*

9. *Ibid.*

10. *Ibid.*, p. 364.

(Matt. 12:34). He said, further, "No one can come to Me, unless the Father who sent Me draws him" (John 6:44). We are free if the Son has made us free, according to John 8:36. James Arminius is clear at this point when he says, "Our will is not free from the first fall; that is, it is not free to good, unless it is made free."[11]

John Wesley taught similarly and, including John Fletcher, says, "We both steadily assert that the will of fallen man is by nature free only to evil."[12]

S. S. White seemed to teach an inclusive fall when he wrote, "Original sin is a condition in which all the faculties of man, understanding, and will, and affections have been perverted. It is a total corruption of the whole human nature."[13] Yet he did not believe that carnality, or original sin, makes the body sinful. However, Paul seems to have taught this when he said, "I see in my members another law at war with the law of my mind and making me captive to the law of sin which dwells in my members" (Rom. 8:11, RSV). The body, also, is included in the complete sanctification which Paul prays that the Thessalonian believers might come to enjoy. He says, "May the God of peace himself sanctify you wholly *[holoteleis]*; and may your spirit and soul and body be kept sound and blameless" (1 Thess. 5:23, RSV).

White (perhaps understandably, because of the era) may have imbibed the Kantian moralism of his principal theology teacher, Drew's Olin Alfred Curtis,[14] and the view of his professors at Chicago University, the bastion of American modernism when White received his Ph.D. degree there in 1939. At any rate, he refuses to admit that fallen natural man is unable to do any good thing.

He argued, "Like God, man is capable of acting consciously toward an end, and aware of the fact that there is a right and wrong between which he can and must choose."[15] He also says,

11. James Arminius, *The Works of James Arminius,* ed. James Nichols (Grand Rapids: Baker Book House, 1956), 1:523.

12. John Wesley, in *A Compend of Wesley's Theology,* ed. Robert W. Burtner and Robert E. Chiles (Nashville: Abingdon Press, 1954), pp. 132-33.

13. White, *Eradication Defined,* pp. 35-36.

14. See his *The Christian Faith* (Grand Rapids: Kregel Publications, n.d.).

15. Stephen S. White, *Essential Christian Beliefs* (Kansas City: Nazarene Publishing House, 1940), p. 27.

"The man who is born in sin still has a sense of right and wrong, still has a capacity for God, and on occasion can do that which is in itself good."[16] He believes firmly that there is a "racial bent to sin,"[17] and that "man is a fallen being,"[18.] but he nudges Wesleyan theology at this point somewhat toward the left of where Wesley was located.

B. *The Human and Its Aberrations*

One whole set of deficiencies that we come by during this life, and that are therefore not nullified when the carnal mind is expelled at the time of our entire sanctification, is prejudices.

Take racial prejudice. It is not inherited from Adam; we do not enter the world with it. We acquire it from our environment. Black children, for example, hear their parents and others speak derisively against whites, and young whites hear blacks bad-mouthed by their parents and others. The "different" appearance of a person of a different race is also a contributing factor. Added to that are differences in culture, training, economic status, ways of expressing faith.

The apostle Peter was prejudiced against Gentiles, and it showed up well after the time of his Spirit baptism at Pentecost. But God gave him a powerful object lesson with the sheet let down from heaven and he was led to confess, "God has shown me that I should not call any man unholy or unclean" (Acts 10:28). The routing of Peter's learned prejudices about the dietary differences between Jews and Gentiles and about God's supposed favoritism towards Peter's kind of folk, the Jews, occurred well after Pentecost.

But that was not the last time he failed to conduct himself consistently under social pressures. He was still subject to mistakes which showed up in too great a desire simply to please people and in inconsistent behavior. That is why, more than 14 years later, Paul needed to help him see this. Paul says, "But

---

16. *Ibid.,* pp. 34-35.
17. *Ibid.,* p. 33.
18. *Ibid.,* p. 32. Related to this, see Robert E. Chiles, *Theological Transition in American Methodism: 1870-1935* (New York: Abingdon Press, 1965). Chiles treats various Methodist theologians from Wesley's time to the time of A. C. Knudson and shows the increasing Pelagianism in Methodist theological history.

when Cephas came to Antioch I opposed him to his face, because he stood condemned. For before certain men came from James, he ate with the Gentiles; but when they came he drew back and separated himself, fearing the circumcision party" (Gal. 2:11-12, RSV).

If Peter's experience at Pentecost did not rout his prejudice against Gentiles, nor his too-great desire to please people, we may suppose that our "Pentecost" will not necessarily nullify such matters either. People today who have had their "Pentecost" might still be prejudiced against certain persons. One might think that no good thing can come from Nazareth; or Arkansas; or staid Vermont; or a liberally oriented denomination; or out of a sharecropper family; or from the Rockefellers; or from the West "where all those cults flourish"; or from women.

If a person today tends to talk too much, or otherwise to act impulsively (like Peter) because of his temperament, entire sanctification will not transform him into a different type of human being. However, with the Holy Spirit indwelling a person in a pervasive fullness, he has a "TelePrompTer" inside to help him more and more to bring his temperament into subjection to God's will.

The same may be said of aberrations of the human nature. If, during this life, and environmentally, human nature gets to be what it ought not to be, we should not expect it to be necessarily corrected at the time of our entire sanctification. At that time, Adamic depravity, which we come into the world with, gets cleansed away. While God might in His graciousness correct some problem we have at any time, it is not necessarily part of the "package" of entire sanctification that these non-Adamic-depravity problems will be corrected immediately. Thus, if a person has come to have homosexual interests, he will of course be enabled not to implement his interests with a partner. This enablement will be given in initial sanctification, at the first work of grace; and there will be added help with the empowerment of one's Pentecost. But the interest might still be present, and it might need to be corrected gradually. Likewise, a person might still have a tendency toward drug or alcohol addiction, and the tendency might be corrected only gradually —although, again, a person is enabled not to implement the tendency, even at the time of initial sanctification.

Entire sanctification is a sanctification, a cleansing, that is entire. No carnality, or original sin, remains to deprave our faculties, to incline us to acts of sin. Carnality has infected, as a fever does, our entire nature, including the body and the reason and the will and the emotions, and carnality is entirely extirpated. This state or condition of a bias, a leaning towards the life of sin, is crucified, destroyed—eradicated, if you please. Even so, entire sanctification is not a panacea; it does not necessarily right the derangements due to aberrating experiences that have happened during this life.

C. *Concluding Observations*

Wesleyans ought to differentiate between carnality and humanity better than sometimes has been done. We ought to mean by carnality, especially that in unbelievers, the entire detriment we receive from Adam's fall. It is original sin, and it consists of a depravity which affects all the aspects of human nature: reason, will, emotions, the body. Because of the Fall, (1) the reason is not trustworthy, making revelation in Scripture and in Christ so imperative; (2) the moral nature is fallen so that we cannot do any good things without the aid of special grace; (3) the emotions are depraved so that our affections are not set on things above but are "inclined toward evil and that continually"; and (4) even our bodies are marred, and need to be cleansed by a sanctification that is entire (1 Thess. 5:23).

We ought to place in the human area whatever is essential to human nature as such—for example, the sex drive, the desire to be appreciated, the desire for self-protection, the various kinds of temperament. The carnal infection of them is extirpated at our entire sanctification, but they remain. In entire sanctification we are cleansed from whatever spiritual detriment we come into the world with (as a result of the fall of Adam) but not necessarily from learned or otherwise acquired mental or emotional or physical aberrations such as have been mentioned above. The Holy Spirit, after our Pentecost, indwells us pervasively, and He helps us not to disobey God willfully due to any of these aberrations, and more and more to become liberated from them—until glorification, when the liberation will become complete.

It follows from this that we ought not to expect overmuch

from the grace of entire sanctification. Neither should we expect too little. It also follows that much charity is called for in our interpersonal relations because, (1) we cannot necessarily tell what are carnal and what are human attitudes and reactions and actions in other persons; and (2) we ought not to expect entire sanctification to extirpate from people immediately the aberrations which have been acquired during a person's life.

To understand entire sanctification, and what to expect God to accomplish in our lives through this second grace is one thing. To experience it is another. The difference is the difference between a painting of a fire and a real fire.

Chapter 8

Receiving and Retaining Entire Sanctification

Although God has provided for our redemption in such a way that, after our justification, we can receive cleansing from original sin through the baptism with the Holy Spirit, we need to cooperate with Him in receiving these and other helps He offers us.

To receive entire sanctification, it is needful for believers to cooperate with God in various ways. Likewise, retaining entire sanctification, as well as receiving it, is important to consider.

A. *Receiving Entire Sanctification*

There is no set formula by which one is assured he will receive entire sanctification. God deals with us as individuals. However, there are basic conditions to be met which are common to all—and everyone must pass through the door of faith.

1. *Understanding what is provided.* An early step toward receiving the second grace is to understand what God's provision is. There are two types of sin, sin as act and sin as racial inclination towards the acts. The acts of disobedience (for which we are personally responsible) need to be forgiven (justification, conversion), but the racial inclination (which we inherited) needs to be cleansed away. Both are made possible because of Jesus Christ's death and resurrection. The blameless Lamb of God, who learned obedience by the things that He suffered,

suffered outside Jerusalem's gates to sanctify the people—all the people—with His own blood (Heb. 13:12).

2. *Preparing ourselves.* The reading of scripture pertaining to entire sanctification is one way to prepare the heart to seek this blessing. Likewise the reading of holiness literature is a help. To hear holiness preaching is a similar benefit—and to hear holiness testimonies. Maintaining an openness before God in prayer so that the Holy Spirit can guide us is fundamental. The holiness writers have had much to say about removing hindrances, too. If the Holy Spirit points out to us some aspect of our lives that is not given over to God, we ask His help in placing it under God's sovereignty. In this preparation, we maintain not only an openness to God in areas known to us, but we must try to be so open that spiritual breakthroughs can occur, as the Spirit spreads new light on our way.

3. *Consecrating ourselves.* As a believer, one yields, or presents himself totally to God (see Rom. 12:1-2; also 6:13), for His use when or where, and in whatever way He wishes. We yield to God our possessions, our talents and proficiencies, our ambitions, our loved ones, our unknown future, ourselves. This is not easy. Charles G. Finney confessed, "I had a great struggle to consecrate myself to God."[1]

A minister questioned D. L. Moody's being invited to his city for an evangelistic campaign, and asked, "Why must we get D. L. Moody to come here? Does he have a monopoly on the Holy Ghost?" The response to him was, "No, but the Holy Ghost has a monopoly on D. L. Moody." Consecration means giving God a monopoly on us.

4. *Exercising faith.* It is faith which precipitates the baptism with the Spirit. As noted previously, the two scripture passages which most clearly state this are Acts 15:9 and Acts 26:18.

Some people like to stress the importance of consecration along with faith as necessary to receiving entire sanctification. That is correct, in a sense, though Wesley laid the major stress on the "by faith alone" aspect. The Nazarene Articles of Faith state this matter well: "Entire sanctification . . . is wrought

---

1. Charles G. Finney, *An Autobiography* (Old Tappan, N.J.: Fleming H. Revell Co., 1876), p. 375.

instantaneously by faith, preceded by entire consecration."[2] In other words, even as repentance precedes justifying faith, consecration precedes sanctifying faith.

Since faith procures entire sanctification, this implies the instantaneous nature of the experience—that it can happen at the very moment, at any moment, when a believer exercises faith. Many believers have gone forward to receive the second blessing, have yielded themselves to God in full consecration, and by faith have entered into their Canaan. It was just like that—no trauma, no delay. The experience was received as uncomplicatedly as forgiveness of sins was.

With others, however, the pace has been slower. They, too, as believers, may have gone forward for prayer, but for all their seeking did not enter into the experience of entire sanctification. The reasons may be many. It may be a drawing back from *complete* consecration. It may be a failure to exercise the necessary faith. It may be because of a lack of understanding. It is natural for the new child of God to want all there is for him in grace, so as soon as he hears of and comes to believe in entire sanctification he becomes a seeker for it. But this might be so early that he does not understand very adequately what he is seeking for, or how to go about it. Thus he might seek without fulfillment.

It has been suggested to some who were struggling to receive the experience that they take it by "dry faith" and announce that it has happened. After all, the Scripture says that when we meet God's conditions, God will sanctify us. But this is hardly adequate advice.

Phoebe Palmer and others developed step-by-step formulas for receiving the second blessing, and no doubt these have helped many people. Perhaps the most widely used one is this three-step technique: (1) put your all on the altar; (2) Christ is the altar; (3) the altar, Christ, sanctifies the gift. Therefore, if the seeker has put all on the altar, he or she is sanctified.

The problem with such methods is that they tend to pro-

---

2. *Manual, Church of the Nazarene,* p. 29. It is also a fact that, while these Articles state that it is wrought by a "baptism" and that it is "wrought instantaneously," they contain no suggestion whatever of a process, or entire sanctification's being gradual. Since no holiness writer I know of, when the Articles were being forged, taught gradual sanctification, I'd guess that what is in the Articles was intentional.

duce superficial seeking without meeting God's conditions. The carnal mind is deceptive (Rom. 7:11) and we might think we are fully consecrated to God when we are not. Merely professing it does not make it so. We are not sanctified wholly, necessarily, when we say we are, but when we indeed are.

The faith which procures entire sanctification is sometimes flashbulblike in its nature. However, it might be an expectant, obedient trust that, when God sees that we have met the conditions He has set, He will sanctify us wholly. As such an expectant trust, faith is durative. For one thing, "faith" is a noun. As such, it is a state of being—and a state of being is durative. If a child has trust in his dad, it is steady and durative. And so might be our faith for entire sanctification.

This durative quality of faith is supportable from Scripture. Jesus once said, "Truly . . . if you have faith, and do not doubt, you . . ." (Matt. 21:21). The word for "doubt" is in the aorist tense, meaning that one simply was not to doubt at all. The word for "faith" is a noun, which of course does not have tense. Yet its auxiliary, "have," does have tense, and its tense, here, is present. This means that faith can be steady. It is a state or condition that can last for an indefinite period of time.

The way "faith" is used, in Scripture, in scores of other passages, also suggests that faith has duration. Jesus exhorted people to "have faith in God" (Mark 11:22), which would have been continuous faith, for "have," again, is in the Greek present tense. Faith could "increase" (Luke 17:5). Stephen was "full of faith" (Acts 6:5). There is an "obedience of faith" (Rom. 1:5). We can "walk in the steps of that faith" (Rom. 4:12). It is something which can "abide" (*menei*, present tense), in a sustained way (1 Cor. 13:13).

This expectant, obedient, trusting faith, which might be present for only an instant before entire sanctification, might also last for two minutes, or two days, or whatever. But when God's conditions are met, and He sanctifies through and through, the faith that He will do this becomes transfigured into knowledge that He has. Then we will receive what Wesley called the witness of the Spirit. When this happens, we will likely not say, "I think (or I believe) that God sanctifies me," but will affirm with assurance, "God sanctifies me."

After faith procures the experience, and the entire sanctification has happened, the experience itself becomes knowledge, and the "we knows" of First John become ours. Then nobody needs to wrest from us a conjured up testimony to the grace of entire sanctification.

B. *The Witness of the Spirit*

After a believer gives himself fully to God and has by faith received the grace of entire sanctification, the Holy Spirit directly witnesses to him that the work of grace has been accomplished. Some holiness writers have suggested that this witness of the Spirit is often received at a later time. Beverly Carradine believed he received the witness three days afterward, and Samuel Logan Brengle some two weeks later. It could well be that the earlier time was when they began decisively to open themselves to this grace, but that the actual entire sanctification occurred at the later time, thus occasioning an immediate witness of the Spirit that it had happened. It is hard to see why something as significant as the baptism with the Holy Spirit should happen, and we would not know about it for three days or two weeks.

Acts 15:8-9 suggests that perhaps right on the heels of our Spirit-baptism, the Holy Spirit bears witness to what has been accomplished. What we have in this passage is not a present participle, which would suggest that the witness is simultaneous with the baptism, but an aorist participle, *dous,* from the common word for "to give," or "to grant," *didomi.* Peter here says, "God, who knows the heart, bore witness to them, giving them the Holy Spirit" (v. 8).

Such an immediate witness is also implied when Paul says, "We have received, not the spirit of this world, but the Spirit who is from God, that we might know the things freely given to us by God" (1 Cor. 2:12). To have "received . . . the Spirit" is no doubt a reference to the Spirit baptism. And among the "things" the Spirit helps us to "know" would be His own presence in the heart of one who has received this baptism.[3]

---

3. There are two special passages which show that we receive the witness of the Spirit to our justification, which are not entirely germane to my purposes here: "The Spirit Himself bears witness with our spirit that we are children of God, . . ." (Rom. 8:16); also, "And because we are sons, God has sent forth the Spirit of His Son into our hearts, crying, 'Abba! Father'" (Gal. 4:6). Since the Spirit witnesses to us our justification, it is likely that He will witness to us our entire sanctification.

The writer of Hebrews makes a strong statement concerning the witness of the Spirit to entire sanctification—and perhaps even to its immediacy. He writes, "By one offering He has perfected for all time[4] those who are sanctified. And the Holy Spirit also bears witness to us" (Heb. 10:14-15).

The numerous "we knows" in First John are importantly supportive, particularly where we read, "We know by this that He abides in us, by the Spirit which He has given us" (1 John 3:24).

It is well known that John Wesley emphasized the witness of the Spirit to both justification and entire sanctification. In fact, entire sanctification and the witness of the Spirit are perhaps the two most distinctive doctrines of Wesley. Wesley wrote sermons on the Spirit's witness, he treated it in his *A Plain Account,* and in many of his letters. In a letter written in 1757 he wrote, "One fruit [of Christian perfection] given at the same instant (at least usually) is a direct, positive testimony of the Spirit that the work is done."[5]

Wesley taught that there is also an indirect witness from the "fruits" of our lives. But the direct witness is primary. He said we should not "rest in any supposed fruit of the Spirit," but seek entire sanctification, and keep on seeking, until the Holy Spirit has witnessed to the grace in our hearts.[6]

Wesley also taught, as has been the usual teaching in the Holiness movement, that the witness of the Spirit, as a direct impression upon our consciousness, might wax and wane. But he added that as we mature to where we are "fathers in Christ" we are likely to experience the consciousness in a more steady way.

C. *Retaining Entire Sanctification*

Wesleyans teach that those who are sanctified wholly might still willfully sin against God and fall away from saving grace. But they still understand entire sanctification to be an "establishing grace," making it much more possible, or perhaps even

---

4. John Wesley, for a time, taught that one could not lose entire sanctification grace, but later revised his view.

5. John Wesley, *The Letters of the Rev. John Wesley,* ed. John Telford (London: The Epworth Press, 1931), 3:213.

6. See Wesley, *Works,* 5:133-34.

likely, that such a person will *retain* his spiritual condition. Once original sin has been expelled through the Spirit baptism, a believer is not double-minded in the way he was following his conversion. Original sin inclines one away from God, so a Christian is better enabled to live the Christlike life once Adamic depravity has been destroyed.

This establishment in grace through entire sanctification is taught in Scripture, a prime passage being 1 Thess. 3:10-13. There Paul, writing to Christian believers, says: "May our God and Father . . . direct our way to you . . . so that He may establish your hearts unblamable in holiness before our God." The KJV and RSV also translate *sterixai* with "establish." The word, an aorist from *histemi,* means "to make to stand . . . to fix . . . to establish, confirm."[7] As aorist in tense, this word suggests that the establishment will occur through a crisis event—else the present or the imperfect tense would have been used.

Besides this, the other verbs that surround this one, and that have to do with the same matter, are also in the aorist tense. The "complete" ("supply," RSV; "perfect," KJV) in 3:10 is aorist, where Paul tells them he wants to "complete what is lacking in your faith." Even though they sound durative, the "increase" and "abound" (KJV), in 3:11-12, are also aorist, so that Paul hopes for a special step-up in their love.

Another important support is Rom. 5:1-5 where Paul writes, "Having been justified by faith, we have peace with God through our Lord Jesus Christ, through whom also we have obtained introduction [admission] by faith into this grace in which we stand" (vv. 1-2). While the "also" and the second "by faith" are not in some of the very old Greek manuscripts, their inclusion, as in NASB, makes good sense context-wise, and they are indeed in some of the respected manuscripts. This seems to speak of a grace beyond justification, in which one is established. This second experience has Pentecost overtones, for Paul speaks of "the love of God [which] has been poured out within our hearts through the Holy Ghost who was given to us" (5:5).

The apostle Peter's experience is also supportive of the fact that the baptism with the Holy Spirit is properly called

---

7. *The Analytical Greek Lexicon,* p. 203.

the establishing grace. Prior to his Pentecost, Peter had been very vocal in his assurances that he would not deny Christ, and yet he soon did. The story of his failure is a familiar one (see John 18:17, 25-27).

Yet after Christ's resurrection and Peter's evident forgiveness for such denials, and after Pentecost had cleansed and empowered him (Acts 2:1-4; 15:8-9; 1:8), Peter is never again all talk and no proof in the showdown. He is now Christ's fearless disciple. In the slammer, he is Christ's. Brought out of jail, and before the "rulers and elders and scribes" Peter is firm. Being "filled with the Holy Spirit" (note the reference to Pentecost), he said to them, "Let it be known to all of you, and to all the people of Israel, that by the name of Jesus Christ, the Nazarene, whom you crucified, whom God raised from the dead—by this name this man stands here before you" (Acts 4:8-10). He concludes by saying, "We cannot stop speaking what we have seen and heard" (Acts 4:20).

And it was that way with the now established Peter—from tight spot to tight spot, from martyrdom to martyrdom among his associates, to what tradition suggests was his own martyrdom by upside-down crucifixion.

The leading writers of the Holiness movement have given extensive treatment to the matter of this "establishing grace," for they considered this to be one of the key results of entire sanctification in the life of the individual. For once original sin, the Adamic propensity to acts of sin, is expelled, a person is measurably helped toward becoming an established Christian. Thomas Cook said that while "absolute security does not belong to this world," still, "holiness secures the safest possible condition on earth."[8]

John Fletcher, Wesley's chief theologian, said that he lost the experience of entire sanctification several times. Yet even Fletcher felt that it contributes to a person's becoming "'strengthened, established, and settled' under his heavenly vine, in the good land that flows with spiritual milk and honey."[9]

Asa Mahan, in his main work, *The Baptism of the Holy*

8. Cook, *New Testament Holiness,* p. 16.
9. John Fletcher, *The Works of the Rev. John Fletcher* (New York: Methodist Episcopal Conference Office, 1836), 2:546.

122 / Entire Sanctification: *The Distinctive Doctrine of Wesleyanism*

Ghost (1870), said, "In reference to the effects of this baptism, we would remark in general, that *permanence and power* are the leading characteristics. Without this, feebleness characterizes the strongest among us; with it, he that is feeble among us is as David."[10]

J. A. Wood, in his widely circulated *Perfect Love* (1880), said: "In order to retain justification, we have to live *obediently,* and that can be done more easily with a pure heart (through entire sanctification) than with an impure one. All things considered, the easiest religious life is the fullest and least obstructed religious life."[11]

Not long afterward, in 1905, C. W. Ruth, an early associate of Bresee, wrote about holiness experience that "while the possibility of backsliding is not removed, the liability of backsliding is reduced to a minimum."[12] Ruth, in his homey way, likened the blessing's preservation qualities to what obtains in the pickling process for preserving food.

This is only a small part of the vast comment in holiness writings on the matter of spiritual establishment through entire sanctification. Let Donald S. Metz be representative when he writes that, although holiness "does not make a person impeccable, . . . [it] makes it less likely that a person will backslide or commit apostasy."[13]

On the matter of the possibility of apostasy, John Wesley himself believed for a time that one could not lose this grace once he had received it, but he later saw evidence enough in the experience of people in his societies to convince him that it can indeed be lost. Phoebe Palmer, in America, also believed that it can be lost, and that often this happens due to a failure to testify to it. (This was Fletcher's explanation of his own backsliding.)

In 1902, Thomas Cook wrote:

> Nearly all who once experienced entire sanctification, and have lost the blessing, are conscious of having refused obedience to some distinct command which came into their life and from which they shrank. Some duty was borne upon them and they knew it to be of God, but they hesitated to

---

10. Mahan, *Baptism of the Holy Ghost,* p. 30.
11. Wood, *Perfect Love,* p. 130.
12. C. W. Ruth, *Bible Readings on the Second Blessing* (Salem: Convention Book Store, 1905), p. 61.
13. Metz, *Studies in Biblical Holiness,* p. 237.

obey. When they left the narrow track of implicit obedience to the leadings of the Spirit, fellowship with God ceased, and the sense of the abiding of the Comforter was gone. Since then a shadow has been over their lives, they have made no progress, and have lacked both power and joy. Nor will they ever find the blessing again until they go back to the place where they dropped the thread of obedience and perform the thing which God then demanded.[14]

A difference of view obtains within the Holiness movement on whether one might lose only the second work of grace, and not the first; or, both, if he experiences spiritual failure. Wesley and Fletcher and Palmer and others have taught that a person can lose the experience of entire sanctification without losing justification. While Scripture gives nothing that is definitive on this question, there is a certain logic to this view. It might well seem that to lose one's entire sanctification all he would need to do would be to negate what he did in order to receive it in the first place. Since no willful act of sin was involved, it might seem that to withdraw this consecration, or to doubt God, would result in a loss of this grace only.

But there are also strong voices on the other side saying that if either is lost, both are lost, and that an act of willful disobedience to God has taken place. This logically calls for basic repentance. The Nazarene *Manual,* reads, "We believe that man, though in the possession of regeneration and entire sanctification, may fall from grace and apostatize and, unless he repent of this, be hopelessly and eternally lost."[15] This says nothing about losing one without losing the other. It only talks about an act of sin, which, if not repented of, would cause us to lose both works of grace because it would mean that we would be eternally lost.

Some in the Holiness movement have taught that a person, who has been sanctified wholly, backslides entirely if at any time he "walks back of the light."[16] Views of this sort, often given out during evangelistic invitations, have damaged the faith of many conscientious people. Baldwin gives a helpful corrective when he writes:

---

14. Cook, *New Testament Holiness,* pp. 140-41.
15. *Manual, Church of the Nazarene,* p. 27.
16. Harmon A. Baldwin, *Holiness and the Human Element* (Kansas City: Beacon Hill Press, 1919), p. 20.

Another declares that if persons are back of the clearest light ever given, if they are not walking unerringly in all the will of God, their grace is all gone, they are backslidden. If the persons who make this statement refer to actual sin against known light, there is no room to question their accuracy, but, strictly speaking, if this claim is true, a man's grace is forfeited every time he fails to pray as much or as often as he should, every time he eats a piece of pie after he feels he has had enough, or every time he speaks an unnecessary word; for are not all these contrary to his highest light?[17]

---

17. *Ibid.*

Chapter 9

Questions Frequently Asked

As a seminary teacher of holiness doctrine for some three decades, and as a convention and church revival preacher, numerous questions on holiness doctrine have been put to me. Since such questions expose the areas of greatest uncertainty or confusion concerning the doctrine, this last chapter will be devoted to answering the more frequently posed queries.

The questions people ask fall into two main categories, those which deal with the experience side and those which relate to holiness doctrine as such.

I. EXPERIENCE-RELATED QUESTIONS

A. *Will prejudices disappear when a person is sanctified wholly?*

Some have taught that prejudices, for example racial ones, will be entirely corrected by the experience of entire sanctification. J. O. McClurkan, a holiness leader of the America's South with Presbyterian background, taught admirably on countless issues, but taught what I feel are extreme views on the matter of prejudices. He wrote, "The sanctified heart is absolutely cleansed of all . . . race prejudice. Holiness deepens and sweetens and broadens the nature until every man of all and every section and nationality and color or condition is loved as a brother. There is no North, no South, no Jew, nor Greek, no Barbarian to the sanctified."[1]

However, since racial, educational, cultural, and other prejudices are learned environmentally, they are not an aspect of Adamic sin, and are not necessarily routed in entire sanctification. As noted earlier in this volume, Peter still had his prejudice against Gentiles well after his Pentecost. God helped this apostle from Capernaum, and He can help us, on such matters. The Holy Spirit, in a full indwelling of us, will prompt us more and more toward loving acts and attitudes. This will help a person to overcome, through spiritual maturation, prejudices such as racial ones.

B. *Will the subconscious be cleansed?*

The late E. Stanley Jones, who was perhaps our century's most widely renowned holiness preacher (along with Paul Rees), taught that at entire sanctification the subconscious—what we now often call the unconscious—is cleansed.

In requested testimony written on a flyleaf for Charles Ewing Brown's thorough and superb *The Meaning of Sanctification,* Jones wrote:

> We live in two minds—the conscious and the subconscious. The subconscious is the residing place of the driving instincts: self, sex, and the herd. . . .
> Into the conscious mind there is introduced at conversion a new life, a new loyalty, a new love. But the subconscious does not obey this new life. . . . There ensues a clash.[2]

Jones goes on to say that "the area of the work of the Holy Spirit is largely, if not entirely, in the subconscious."[3] He says further, "I found that if I would surrender . . . He would cleanse at these depths. . . . I surrendered and accepted the gift by faith."[4]

This all sounds beautiful. But it mines in the area of psychology and not in the area of Bible and theology. It suggests an equating of the subconscious with original sin. Yet this can-

---

1. *Zion's Outlook,* February 7, 1901, p. 8. See Timothy L. Smith, *Called unto Holiness* (Kansas City: Nazarene Publishing House, 1962), p. 183, for numerous other references to McClurkan's views at this point.
2. See Brown, *Meaning of Sanctification,* p. ii.
3. *Ibid.*
4. *Ibid.*

not be. The subconscious is not what we come into the world with, which is what original sin is. The subconscious, insofar as it still enjoys respect in the schools, has to do with what is packed into our inner minds during this life—often by aberrating experiences. From it our dreams arise. In it are a thousand thousand memories. It is why, for example, we often have unwilled hostility feelings toward authority figures.

If the subconscious were cleansed in entire sanctification, we would be cleansed of far more than the Adamic sin we come into the world with. If it were cleansed away at that time, entire sanctification would have done more wonders than is obvious with all of us sometimes kooky holiness people. If it were cleansed, surely we would never dream of doing what, in our conscious minds, we would not do. Yet we do so dream, at times.

Entire sanctification is a sanctification, a cleansing, that is entire. No original sin remains to deprave our faculties, to incline us to acts of sin. Carnality, a state or condition that is a bias against God, and constitutes a leaning toward the life of sin, is crucified, destroyed, "eradicated"—as the Nazarene Articles of Faith on original sin states. Even so, entire sanctification is not a panacea; it does not right the sundry derangements due to aberrating experiences that have happened during this life. These become corrected gradually as we grow in grace, and they become fully corrected only when our "mortality puts on immortality"—only when the sanctified are glorified.

C. *Will an experience of entire sanctification result in personality integration?*

There is admittedly a certain degree of personality integration when the dividedness due to the carnal mind is dissolved. Yet it is surely too much to say, simply, as some have, that holiness is the integrating experience.[5] Still, there are many conflicts stemming from the human nature. These are overcome only through growth in grace, as God helps us deal with them, one by one.

---

5. Donald Metz lists as "among the results of entire sanctification in the area of personality integration," "a sense of self-worth," a consistent personality which is displayed in all relationships, and "an absence of inner spiritual conflicts" (see his *Studies in Biblical Holiness*, p. 254).

D. Will impatience be conquered?

J. A. Wood includes "impatience" as one of the "fruits of inbred sin."[6] If it is indeed one of those fruits, then, when a believer has been cleansed from inbred sin in entire sanctification, his impatience ought to be gone. But impatience might arise, for example, from a natural drive for superior accomplishment which is not realized, or from an organic reaction in a young mother of several fretful children.

In this connection, J. A. Wood said of those sanctified wholly that "the quiet of their spirit is untouched, and they are never destitute of peace."[7] Yet would this necessarily be so for a young mother with small children, whose husband has absconded, and whose bills are past due and cannot be paid, and whose children are fretful because their father is gone?

And is it realistic for him to say that "the quiet of their spirit is untouched"? Untouched when a spouse leaves with infatuation for another person? Untouched when the boss, based on incorrect information, says "You're fired"? Untouched when a son or daughter is killed in an automobile accident on his or her high school graduation night? If the quiet of our spirits is untouched by such experiences, we would be robots—not humans. Scripture surely does not advertise any work of grace that automatically works wonders such as this.

Wound the sanctified and they bleed. Grown men among them might hurt big, and even aloud. It is not that their spirits are "untouched." It is that when they are down, on their backs, and the count is just about up, they know whose they are and to whom they can go for refuge.

E. Will a person be freed from improper desires?

R. T. Williams, early Nazarene general superintendent, in his *Temptation: A Neglected Theme,*[8] taught correctly that improper desires are not inconsistent with the holiness life. He said that sin is committed only when one wills to implement a sinful desire, which correctly interprets the meaning of the

---

6. Wood, *Perfect Love,* p. 124.
7. *Ibid.,* p. 127.
8. R. T. Williams, *Temptation: A Neglected Theme* (Kansas City: Nazarene Publishing House, 1920).

Book of James: "Each one is tempted when he is carried away and enticed by his own lust. Then when lust [strong desire] has conceived, it gives birth to sin" (Jas. 1:14-15). Thus when a strong desire for what is sinful becomes united to a person's will to do it, then and only then is sin conceived. The original desire is an injection from without or perhaps a purely physical impulse. Our response to it is what is morally significant.

In the process of an act of sin there are perhaps several steps before a person would be guilty of disobedience to God. There is (1) the attention given to what is wrong; (2) then the desire for that; (3) then perhaps even a pre-volitional impulse toward what is desired; and (4) finally a person's judgment which turns on the red light of danger. If, at that point, a person does not will to do what he has desire to do, he has not sinned. God has helped him to be victorious. He has been tempted in a real way, but has not disobeyed God.

F. *Will all our motives be pure after entire sanctification?*

Entire sanctification does not make all our motives pure, as has too often been taught in the Holiness movement. Carnality, original sin, is cleansed away in the second work of grace, so our motives are not carnal. They are not sinful. Yet they are not necessarily pure—not necessarily the best, or fully acceptable, or even approved by God.

Motives are inward bases or springboards for doing what we do. They can indeed stem from the carnal nature, but they can also stem from the human nature. Insofar as they stem from the human nature, in those sanctified wholly, they might or might not be "pure" or proper.

Entire sanctification does not dehumanize us. This has always been taught in holiness circles. This means that the various human desires or "instincts" are still basically what they previously were, only cleansed of their carnal infection. Thus, for example, the desire to be appreciated is still there. So with other normal desires.

The desire to be with other persons is still there. If a person were gregarious before entire sanctification, he should not expect to be any different after his Pentecost. He might still have his preferences as to where he would like to work for Christ, though God might have other plans for him which he must be amenable to.

A person might be inwardly motivated toward a direction in his life that would be safe. The desire for self-preservation is natural; it is human. This desire to avoid the hazardous might motivate a person to be less than sacrificial in his service for Christ. The human in us, our "instinctive" desires, might inwardly motivate us in a direction that is not God's first choice for us. Growth in grace often needs to occur, even after entire sanctification, before our motives are pure in the sense of being correct in God's eyes.

"The altar was filled with seekers. As soon as the invitation was given, people started coming forward to accept Christ." This is sometimes the way a person might report to a friend or to a congregation on a service he has helped to conduct. If such a report is given solely in order to bring God glory—probably with a disclaimer of one's own power to produce such effects— there is no problem concerning the motive.

Reports of this sort, however, might be given even by a person who is sanctified wholly, in order to be better appreciated by his hearers. Since it is only human to desire to be appreciated, such reporting does not necessarily mean that the person is lacking in spiritual grace. It would certainly mean, however, that he needs to grow in grace a bit, so that the human desire to be appreciated would be kept subservient to the desire to bring God glory. The motive would not be carnal, but it still would not be pure—in the sense of being acceptable to God.

After entire sanctification, then, our motives are not carnal. They are pure in that sense, but only in that sense. In the wider context of being pure—acceptable to God—they might not be pure. Growth in grace might need to take place before our humanity is brought fully under the sovereignty of Christ.

II. DOCTRINE-RELATED QUESTIONS

A. *Why are there two works of grace?*

Some holiness writers have had such a penchant for finding two works of grace taught in Scripture that they have given unsound bases for the two distinct steps in our redemption. Beverly Carradine based his teaching of two works of grace, in part, on the fact that there are two covenants, the Old Testament one and the New Testament one. Of these two covenants he wrote, "These two covenants embrace all that God does for the soul on earth, and accurately describe the two works of grace, regeneration and sanctification."[9]

Carradine's analogy is not too bad for, after all, there are two dispensations, and the Holy Spirit was poured out upon believers approximately when the second dispensation began. But both works of grace could have occurred during the Old Testament dispensation, although such was not prevalent. (Note Isaiah 6; Psalm 51.)

However, on the basis that there are two works of grace because there are two covenants, it would logically follow that we could not now be justified, since we are not under the Old Testament covenant, the time when people could become justified. We could now receive only our own dispensation's kind of grace: entire sanctification. This, of course, is not the case.

The beginning of the new dispensation predates Pentecost, for it began with the birth of Christ and, according to the Book of Hebrews, with Christ's becoming himself a high priest and, on the Cross, making a sacrifice of himself for our sins. Hebrews makes very much of the two covenants which are similar time-wise to the two dispensations, but it does not suggest that the second one began quite as late as at Pentecost.

The special doctrinal reason why there are two works of grace is because there are two types of sin: our own acts of sin, and the Adamic sin we are born with. Another reason is a psychological one: we are in a different frame of mind when we are rebels against God seeking forgiveness than when we are children of God who are yielding ourselves to Him for His using us. Yet the most unanswerable basis for there being two works of grace is because it is taught in Scripture, as presented earlier in this volume.

B. *Is it correct to say that "the old man" is original sin?*

One of the most widespread, yet inadequate interpretations of scripture by holiness writers is interpreting what Paul calls the "old man" as original sin.

Only Paul uses the term, in the New Testament, and he, only three times. It quite certainly refers to the old, unregenerate life, the kind of person that obtained before conversion.

---

9. Carradine, *Second Blessing in Symbol*, p. 87.

This, in contrast to the new man, the person of the new birth, the regenerate person. There was perhaps not a single one of the early holiness books which opposed the position that the "old man" is original sin. Men like B. W. Huckabee,[10] Beverly Carradine,[11] C. W. Ruth,[12] and H. C. Morison made unequivocal statements to that effect. Morrison writes: "The casting out of the 'old man,' the plucking up of the root of bitterness, the destruction of the body of sin, the *eradication* of the carnal mind, the purging out of 'the sin that dwelleth in me,' are all one and the same thing, which is accomplished by the instantaneous baptism with the Holy Ghost, purifying the heart by faith."[13]

Authors who have enjoyed special respect as theologians have also taught in this way. A. M. Hills said that "there are several other names applied to this 'old man' by God; but the list is quite extended enough to describe him sufficiently for recognition. In common speech we call him 'DEPRAVITY.' He is best known among men by that name."[14] In another book Hills says, "In view of the context, can such a crucifixion and dying mean anything less than that 'the sin,' 'the old man' of depravity, can be so destroyed by sanctifying grace that the Christian can become as dead to any internal impulse to sin as a corpse is dead to the attractions of the world that once charmed him?"[15]

S. S. White helped to popularize this view in recent decades. He wrote, "In this pre-sanctified state, man does not commit deliberate acts of sin. He is saved, not from the presence, but from the power of the carnal mind. Thus the 'old man of sin' is kept under or suppressed."[16] Much earlier, Adam Clarke had taken the same kind of view. He wrote, "We find

10. Huckabee, *Carnal Mind* (no publisher, n.d.), p. 8.
11. B. Carradine, *The Old Man* (Noblesville, Ind.: Newby Book Room, 1965, reprint of 1896 edition by Kentucky Methodist Publication Co.).
12. C. W. Ruth, *The Second Crisis in Christian Experience* (Chicago: Christian Witness Co., 1913), p. 59.
13. Morrison, *Baptism with the Holy Ghost,* p. 24.
14. Hills, *Pentecost Rejected,* p. 72. See related matters on pp. 25, 31, 63-64, 69.
15. A. M. Hills, *The Establishing Grace* (Kansas City: Nazarene Publishing House, 1937), p. 30.
16. White, *Eradication Defined,* p. 45.

that *ho palaios hemon anthropos,* 'our *old man,*' used here [in Romans 6:6], and in Eph. iv. 22, and Coloss. iii. 9, is the same as . . . what we mean by *indwelling sin,* or the *infection of nature,* in consequence of the *fall.*"[17] And still somewhat earlier, John Wesley himself at least sometimes took this kind of position. In his *Notes,* at Rom. 6:6, he says, of "our old man": "Coeval with our being, and as old as the Fall; our evil nature; a strong and beautiful expression for that entire depravity and corruption which by nature spreads itself over the whole man, leaving no part uninfected."[18]

Although these and others equate the "old man" with original sin, the view is really not supportable. Take first the Rom. 6:6 instance of the phrase "old man." In the *American Standard Version* we read: "Knowing this, that our old man is crucified with *him,* that the body of sin might be destroyed." The KJV has "old man" also, whereas the RSV and NASB have "old self" here.

The interpretation revolves around the Greek word *hina* which almost always means "in order that" (the exceptions being its occurrence in Matt. 10:25; John 4:34; 6:29; 1 John 4:17; 5:3, etc.). It is therefore often called "the *hina* of purpose." In a Greek passage, what is referred to following this word is different from what is referred to just before it. The same is so, of course, with the English "in order that," which translates *hina.* The gracious God does not do something for us in order that He might do the same thing for us. But if the "old man" is original sin, and if "the body of sin" is original sin, then Rom. 6:6 states that our original sin is crucified in order that original sin might be destroyed, which is a redundancy. If, however, our "old man" refers to the old, unregenerate life, as different from the new life in Christ, that is, the new birth (the "newness of life" mentioned at the end of Rom. 6:4), then Paul is saying that we are regenerated in order that we might be sanctified wholly. This is a logical sequence.

This interpretation also saves us from having to add a word or a thought to what Paul says on both sides of the *hina.* Since Paul cannot be saying that we are sanctified wholly in

---

17. Clarke, *Clarke's Commentary,* 6:77.
18. John Wesley, *Explanatory Notes upon the New Testament* (London: Epworth Press, 1941, reprint), p. 540.

order to be sanctified wholly, most Wesleyans have thought of Paul as saying that we have been sanctified wholly *provisionally* through Christ's death in order to be sanctified wholly *experientially*. If, however, we interpret the "old man" as being the old, unregenerate life, we do not need to add "provisionally" before the *hina* and something like "experientially" to the later clause. To me, Paul is saying that our unregenerate self is crucified as surely as Christ on the Cross was crucified, and that God brings about this death to the former life in order that the state of original sin might also be destroyed.

Also if "our old man" refers to original sin, or the body or state of sin, why did Paul not use a pronoun the second time around? Why did he say that our old man is crucified, provisionally if you please, in order that *it* might be destroyed in actuality when we as believers trust God for such?

This view strengthens the passage as a holiness text, since it sees both works of grace mentioned in one verse—and such passages tend to be stronger supports for entire sanctification teaching than separated passages in which the two works of grace are taught in a disjoined way.

In Eph. 4:19-25 this "old man" or "old self" is equated with their "former manner of living." Also the term is used in Col. 3:9; but it should be noted that here both carnal affections and acts of sin are connected with the "old man," which would add support to the view that the phrase more accurately refers to the unregenerate life instead of simply original sin.

C. Should we call original sin "self-will" and "rebellion"?

To call original sin "self-will" is not quite appropriate. The expression suggests that we are talking about a person's own will in distinction from, and perhaps opposed to, God's will. Any will of that sort—one's own will instead of God's—is taken care of through God's forgiveness at the first work of grace. If, after our conversion, we still have self-will, the conversion would not have been very real. So to give that name to original sin is to suggest an undermining of the first work of grace. Bertha Munro's term, "self-willedness," is preferable.

The problem with the similar term "rebellion" is the same. It suggests an undercutting of what God does for us in the first work of grace. Certainly a truly regenerate person would not be in rebellion against God's will.

Actually, in both the Old Testament and the New, numerous generic and metaphoric and concrete-act words for sin occur in the Hebrew and Greek. The most serious acts of all seem to be the rebellious ones. They are worse than sin as missing the mark, as missing the way, as ungodliness, as unrighteousness, or whatever. *Pesha* is the commonest of these words in the Old Testament for sin as rebellion.

In the New Testament it is the same way. Laying aside the generic words for sin such as those that refer to what is evil or wicked, you have metaphors for acts of sin. The most frequent of these metaphors is *hamartia,* appearing, with all its cognates, some 270 times. But when you want to get right down to the worst of all these types of sin-acts, there is the rarely used *parabasis,* for "transgression," a word that is utterly serious in the way the Hebrew *pesha* is. If there is not any law that one knows he is willfully breaking, he is not guilty of any "transgression" according to Rom. 4:15. One does not usually rebel against a peer, but against a superior—perhaps against a king; more likely, against God himself.

So it is better to avoid calling original sin rebellion. Rebellion sounds like *rebellion* which might characterize a rebel against God but surely not the regenerate but not-yet-sanctified-wholly children of our Holy God.

D. *Are "surrender" and "consecrate" the same?*

Many holiness people use "surrender" as a synonym for "consecrate." Believers, who are already children of God, are exhorted to surrender themselves to God and let Him sanctify them wholly.

This, again, is a practice which tends to undermine regeneration. It states that people who are already God's people need to surrender to Him. Yet to surrender is what a rebel does. It is what one does if he has broken the civil law and reports himself to the authorities. It is what a rebel army does in war. To surrender, in the spiritual sense, is what we do to be forgiven of our sins.

There might be a meaning of "surrender" that is a bit lighter than what a rebel or a criminal or an enemy army does, but the usual meaning is the one mentioned. The word is not a synonym of "consecrate."

If one were to say that Japan consecrated itself to General MacArthur, or that the bank robber consecrated himself to the police, it would have in it a smidgen of the ridiculous.

The word "yield" *is* an acceptable synonym of "consecrate," although it is closer in meaning to what a rebel might do than "consecrate" is.

E. *Should we say that the self is crucified when we are sanctified wholly?*

Holiness people are often told that in entire sanctification the self is crucified. Related to this, we are told that original sin is selfishness when, actually, what seems to be selfishness might often be the outcropping of something like being or having been an overindulged child.

Galatians 2:20 has been used to support this, where we read, "I have been crucified with Christ; and it is no longer I who live, but Christ lives in me." A related passage is Gal. 6:14, which Daniel Steele calls a "reciprocal crucifixion." Paul says: "May it never be that I should boast, except in the cross of our Lord Jesus Christ, through which the world has been crucified to me, and I to the world."

Some holiness writers view these passages as referring to what happens at regeneration. This might be indicated in the latter passage which suggests a conversion-like break with the world that Paul is speaking of. If one as a Christian has not broken with the world in the sense of the sphere where God is opposed, he is hardly a Christian. The world, outside the church, pretty much breaks with a person—and he with it—when he surrenders his rebel heart to God and receives God's gracious forgiveness. Then, if the figure of crucifixion may be expected to be used in the same way by the same writer in the same Epistle, that might be what is meant by the Gal. 2:20 passage.

On either interpretation, with Gal. 2:20, one must do a bit of exegetical gymnastics. One cannot interpret it literally since "I" is crucified, and yet an "I" lives. The usual holiness interpretation is probably correct, that it refers to the second work of grace. Even so, if that is the way one views it, it is not quite correct to say that the self is crucified in entire sanctification. If Paul is saying that self is crucified, he wastes no time in saying that the same self still lives.

It is better to say that the carnal infection of the self is crucified—its self-centeredness—but not the self—not the self itself. Instead of the self itself's being crucified, anything but that is happening. The carnal mind that has clung like a barnacle to the self (as Romans 7 suggests) is crucified, and the self itself, instead of being crucified, is trued up—made a truer self than it was when it was infected (as in the case of a fever) by the carnal mind.

F. *Is it correct to call entire sanctification the cleansing experience?*

By so referring to the second grace we imply that there is no cleansing at the first work of grace. Yet there is indeed a cleansing in the conversion experience. At that time, as discussed in an earlier chapter, we are justified, when God as judge forgives us, absolving us of our guilt (Rom. 5:1). We are also regenerated, born anew—from above, born again (John 3:5). And we are reconciled (2 Cor. 5:18)—the two estranged parties, God and the rebel, being made compatible. That is why we can then be adopted into God's family as His children (John 1:12; Rom. 8:15-16; 1 John 3:1).

But about in the midst of these concurrent happenings, we also receive a cleansing, often called initial sanctification. It is a cleansing of the propensity to acts of sin which builds up in us somewhat habitually because of our acts of sin. If we commit acts of sin, rebelling against God in this way and in that way, day after day, year after year, a tendency builds up in us to keep on doing these willful acts. We do them more and more easily, as a way of life. There is little sweating over one more act of sin as it is decided upon. Very little of the trauma is present that we felt when we first started saying no to God.

All this is in part the reason why, in church work, we try to get children and young people to turn to God and be saved. In those green and growing years, before there is any great build-up of this acquired depravity through acts of sin, it is easier for a person to repent, changing his mind about the life of sin.

If, at our conversion, we were forgiven of only our acts of

sin, but not cleansed of the tendency to them that has built up in us, we could not live a Christian life. We would no doubt go right back to the life of sin that we had been living, in spite of the Holy Spirit's persuading helps. But God knows what we need. He not only forgives us of our past sins, He cleanses us of this acquired bias to them. This is the "washing of regeneration" referred to in Tit. 3:5.

At a later time, as one learns about God's full plan of redemption, he needs to consecrate himself to God and, by faith (again), receive cleansing from his Adamic propensity to acts of sin. This later cleansing we call entire sanctification. At this time the Adamic inclination of sin is cleansed away (Acts 15: 8-9), destroyed (Rom. 6:6), crucified (Gal. 5:24). John Wesley liked especially to say that this state or condition is "expelled." This cleansed experience is often called purity of heart (Matt. 5:8). The carnal mind (Rom. 8:1-9), indwelling sin (Rom. 7:17, 20), sometimes called "the sin" (often in Romans 6), is dealt with decisively. In the Holiness movement we used to say that this sin is eradicated. If we do not very often use that word anymore, since it seemed to suggest to many people that we thought of sin as in some sense physical, we today mean by cleansing precisely what was and is meant by eradication.

To sum up, there is cleansing in both works of grace, and since there is cleansing in the first (conversion), it is not quite correct to call the second work of grace the cleansing experience.

G. *Should we say that Jesus saves and the Holy Spirit sanctifies?*

This implies that Jesus accomplishes for us the first work of grace and that the Holy Spirit accomplishes the second work of grace. This is not a gross error, yet it is not quite correct. This is because each of the three Persons of the Trinity figures in a signal way in both of the works of God's grace.

Take the first work of grace—conversion, sometimes called salvation. Jesus Christ, the Second Person of the Trinity, provides for the forgiveness of our acts of sin by His death and resurrection. He gave His life a ransom for us (Mark 10:45).

He "was put to death for our trespasses and raised for our justification" (Rom. 4:25, RSV). The just for the unjust, He died for our sins, and God the Father raised Him from the dead on that first Easter morning. His death propitiated, assuaged, softened God's holy wrath directed against us as rebels, making it possible for God the Father to justify us and still be himself just (Rom. 3:23-26).

"For our sake he made him to be sin who knew no sin, so that in him we might become the righteousness of God" (2 Cor. 5:21, RSV).

The Holy Spirit also figures in a signal way in the first work of grace. He "convinces" us of sin and of the righteousness that is offered us, and also of the fact of the judgment to come (John 16:8-11, RSV). This is called prevenient grace in which the Holy Spirit approaches us and initiates in us even the first faint yearning for God. Without this, we would be "inclined to evil and that continually" as so many creeds put it. Christ loved us and gave himself for us; and the Holy Spirit, both by direct impressions and through numerous instrumentalities, reminds us of what has been provided for us. Long ago He inspired people to write the Holy Scriptures, which are able to make us wise regarding salvation (2 Tim. 3:15). He calls and anoints persons who preach and who otherwise witness to sinners of God's offer of forgiveness.

God the Father also figures strategically in a person's conversion. He laid out the plan of salvation from the very foundation of the world. He so loved the whole world that He sent His Son among us, finally to die on a Roman cross outside the gates of Jerusalem. Most significantly, He is the one who forgives us, since it is the Holy Father that we peculiarly offend by our acts of sin. In an isolated way, there is a suggestion in the New Testament that Jesus has the power to forgive sins. Since He tells us He could do no great works, such as healings, on His own part, and that it was the Father who actually did them (John 5:36), it might be that Jesus had the power to forgive sins as a power which the Father delegated to Him. When we now, at the altar or elsewhere, ask Jesus to forgive us of our sins, it is actually God the Father who forgives us. So God the Father, God the Son, and God the Holy Spirit, the three Persons in the Godhead, all figure significantly in the first work of grace.

Now to the second work of grace. Holiness people generally believe that it is the Holy Spirit who sanctifies believers as a second crisis in Christian experience. George Allen Turner, on this matter, without necessarily deploring the fact, says: "Some works on systematic theology treat sanctification under the section of the Holy Spirit. This illustrates the widespread belief that, as Christ is the basis of one's justification, so the Spirit is the agent in his sanctification."

Although, as Turner says, the belief is widespread, it is not quite correct. All three Persons of the Trinity figure significantly in a believer's entire sanctification, just as in his conversion. Jesus died on the Cross to provide for this and all other aspects of God the Father's grace. The Christ who visited us for our redemption, the Son of Righteousness who rose "with healing in His wings," who mediates between the Father and us, provides for prevenient, forgiving, sanctifying, providential, miraculous grace, and for other kindnesses toward us on the Holy Father's part. Specifically on sanctification, we read in Hebrews that Christ, "that He might sanctify the people through His own blood, suffered outside the gate" (13:12). Also, it is Jesus who baptizes believers with the Holy Spirit, effecting entire sanctification. John the Baptizer stated that he baptized with water but that One was coming afterward, Jesus, who would baptize people with the Holy Spirit (see Matt. 3:11-12).

Scripture also describes God the Father's function in our entire sanctification. Paul told the Thessalonian believers, "This is the will of God, your sanctification" (1 Thess. 4:3, RSV), so the Father wills it. But it seems to be the Father who actually does this cleansing work in believers, for we read, "May the God of peace himself sanctify you wholly" (1 Thess. 5:23, RSV).

The Holy Spirit helps us to receive what Christ provides for and what the Father actually grants us, in entire sanctification as well as in justification. And we are baptized by Christ with the Holy Spirit. Two or three times, in Scripture, the Holy Spirit is said to do the sanctifying, as when Paul says, "I have written very boldly to you on some points, so as to remind you again, because of the grace that was given me from God, to be a minister of Christ Jesus to the Gentiles, ministering as a priest the gospel of God, that *my* offering of the Gentiles might be acceptable, sanctified by the Holy Spirit" (Rom. 15:15-16).

Because, then, all three Persons of the Trinity figure strategically in both works of grace, we tend to be a bit incorrect when we say that Jesus saves and that the Holy Spirit sanctifies.

H. Why should we speak of this second work of grace as the baptism WITH the Holy Spirit?

There is a touch of theological error in the widely used phrase "the baptism *of*" (instead of "with") the Holy Spirit. In the early history of the Holiness movement, "of," instead of "with," was in widespread use. Asa Mahan titled his 1870 book *The Baptism of the Holy Ghost,* and that book was the major one on the subject for some time. Mahan (and the magazine *Guide to Holiness*) popularized this wording, with "of," so that, even after holiness people were becoming much more Wesleyan than Mahan was on original sin and its cleansing, they were often still using his wording. Even W. B. Godbey titled his book *Baptism of the Holy Ghost* (which has no date on it but which was probably published after 1906 because he talks considerably about the tongues-speaking people who flourished after that date).

Jack Ford, in *What the Holiness People Believe,* issued as recently as 1954, uses this kind of wording, as have numerous other publications even in recent times.

It might seem that the difference between two prepositions, "of," and "with," would be a "small potatoes" matter indeed. The fact is, however, that it makes a world of theological and biblical difference.

If we use "of," we are saying that this is the Holy Spirit's baptism. If we use "with," we are saying that this is Christ's baptism, not now using water as John the Baptist did, but "using," in a sense, the Holy Spirit.

And actually it is not the Holy Spirit's own baptism. It is Christ's baptism, in which the agent is not water, but the Holy Spirit.

The "with" is the way Scripture words it. John had baptized with water, but he said one was to come afterward who would "baptize . . . with the Holy Spirit" (Matt. 3:11).

I. Does Romans 7 depict a person who is in a regenerate state?

Occasionally, holiness writers have interpreted Romans 7 as describing a regenerate person. W. B. Godbey did, as have a few others, such as the great holiness preacher H. C. Morrison.[19]

Much more widespread than in the holiness literature is the folk theology in which the passage is presented in this way by ministers and teachers. However, this is an inadequate interpretation of Scripture. Anyone in the Holiness movement knows that a regenerate person does not sin willfully, and yet this person depicted in Romans 7 seems to do that. In v. 15 the writer says, "I am not practicing what I *would* like *to do,* but I am doing the very thing I hate." And he says in v. 18: "I know that nothing good dwells in me, that is, in my flesh; for the wishing is present in me, but the doing of the good *is* not."

Verses 12 and 22 appear, on the surface, to suggest that a regenerate person is being described. But in Wesleyanism we have long interpreted them in the light of our doctrine of prevenient grace. In v. 12 Paul writes, "So then, the Law is holy, and the commandment is holy and righteous and good." An unregenerate person is inclined to evil and that continually, apart from prevenient grace which God gives to him even as a rebel. But with this grace, even without his being saved, he might well recognize that God's law is holy—and altogether desirable. We often find such as this today. A person might not be a Christian, but if prevenient grace is significantly operative in him, he might well be glad that a church is in his community, with its clergyman and its saving influences.

A similar attitude is expressed by this person in v. 22: "I joyfully concur with the law of God in the inner man." Some have suggested that this is similar to the righteous man's delighting in God's law in Psalm 1. Yet that person is said to be righteous. In v. 22, the concurring with or delighting in God's law is not after the new man, but only according to the inner man. James Arminius is correct in suggesting that everyone has an inner man, in distinction from the outward man of

---

19. Morrison in *Baptism with the Holy Ghost,* p. 24, wrote: "Observe here that the inward man *delights in the law of God.* The sinner has no inward man except the 'old man,' and you may be sure the 'old man' does not delight in the law of God. The inward man spoken of here is the regenerated man, the new man, imparted by the grace of God to the penitent sinner by regenerating grace, at the time of his justification. This *new 'inward man,'* delights in the law of God, but the 'old man' remaining in the nature makes war on the *new man,* and when the new man would do good, the 'old man,' (evil) is present with him, to hinder him in carrying out his good intentions."

the body. And an unregenerate person, who might be profoundly inclined toward God by prevenient grace, might well say that he joyfully concurs with God's law.

Holiness people have often noted that Paul refers to indwelling sin in vv. 17 and 20 of this chapter, where, respectively, Paul speaks of "sin which indwells me," and "sin which dwells in me." This they have correctly interpreted as references to original sin. On this basis they have then suggested that this passage describes a regenerate person who is befuddled by original sin. Yet an unregenerate person also is troubled by original sin—not just the regenerate person. But this person seems to be unregenerate because, as has been pointed out, he implies in vv. 15 and 18 that he willfully sins against God.

Paul here is using the "historical present," that is, actually, the present tense, as a lively way of describing his earlier experience as an unregenerate person who strove to keep God's law but found that he was forever failing in the attempt. One reason for this interpretation that Paul was describing an earlier experience, is because in the chapter immediately following he seems to enjoy victory—just the opposite of chapter 7. Romans 8 opens with Paul saying: "There is therefore now no condemnation for those who are in Christ Jesus. For the law of the Spirit of life in Christ Jesus has set you ['me,' in KJV, RSV] free from the law of sin and death" (vv. 1-2). Also, vv. 8-9 seem to show that the bondage of sin described in Romans 7 does not exist. Paul says that "those who are in the flesh cannot please God" (v. 8). This "flesh" seems to be the indwelling sin and the "law of sin" referred to in Romans 7. Then, in v. 9 Paul says, "However you are not in the flesh but in the Spirit if indeed the Spirit of God dwells in you." Since one of the rules in the science of interpreting Scripture is that a writer does not contradict himself in the same document, we get Romans 7 and Romans 8 into agreement with each other by suggesting that Romans 8 is his present experience and that Romans 7 depicts his previous experience.

J. Do Catholics teach purgatorial entire sanctification?

A widely disseminated error associated with holiness teaching is the idea that the Roman Catholics say we receive entire sanctification in purgatory. John Wesley himself suggested this, and it has been parroted by Wesleyans for two centuries. In his widely used *A Plain Account of Christian Perfection* he writes, "Some say, 'This [Christian perfection] cannot be attained till we have been refined by the fire of purgatory.'" Wesley went on to suggest that others say "it will be attained as soon as the soul and the body part." Also, he mentions his own view, that it "'may be attained before we die.'"[20]

Many people have picked up Wesley's breakdown of the three views, including the matter of purgatorial entire sanctification, and have put it into countless books and magazines. Outstanding scholars such as S. S. White did it. P. P. Belew's *The Case for Entire Sanctification,* published in the 1970s says: "Another view, held by the Roman Catholic church, is that the believer is sanctified after death by the love-fires of purgatory."[21]

The Roman Catholics do not teach this. They teach that original sin is cleansed when a person receives water baptism—this usually being when one is an infant. The guilt of original sin is washed away at that time, and if an infant dies without water baptism, he is to go into limbo, an eternal state of neither bliss nor torment. They teach that one receives the Holy Spirit in a special way at Confirmation, usually 10 years or so later, which is somewhat similar to the Spirit baptism of holiness doctrine. Purgatory, as they say, is for purging a person of guilt accruing to him for venial sins—and the temporal guilt from mortal sins.

K. *Do Wesleyans teach "Holiness or Hell"?*

Occasionally it has been taught or implied that if a believer is not sanctified wholly he will go into perdition if he dies. This is largely based on the Heb. 12:14 passage: "Pursue . . . the sanctification ["holiness," KJV] without which no one will see the Lord." W. B. Huckabee said: "It is every whit as dangerous for the believer to wait until death to be sanctified, as it is for the sinner to wait until death to be saved. There is as much reason in the one as in the other."[22]

---

20. Wesley, *Plain Account*, p. 3.
21. P. P. Belew, *The Case for Entire Sanctification* (Kansas City: Beacon Hill Press of Kansas City, 1974), p. 24.
22. Huckabee, *The Carnal Mind*, p. 58.

W. B. Godbey wrote an entire book entitled *Holiness, or Hell?* In it he teaches this kind of option. In another book, *The Incarnation of the Holy Ghost,* Godbey implies the holiness-or-hell teaching. Of entire sanctification he says, "This makes you a *bona fide* citizen of grace in this world, which is the preparatory for the kingdom of glory in heaven, as a qualification for which you must have the old bitter root and poisonous seed of sin eradicated out of the heart by the cleansing blood, sprinkled by the Holy Ghost."[23]

George D. Watson also seemed to teach holiness or hell. He wrote, "Pardon and purity are both received by separate, specific acts of receptive faith; . . . are both retained by constant submission, . . . are both requisite to a happy, useful life, and both *absolutely essential* to admission to heaven."[24]

Such teaching, however, is more congenial to Roman Catholic and Reformed theology than it is to Wesleyan doctrine. As just mentioned, Roman Catholics teach that if a baby is not baptized, so as to cleanse it of the guilt of original sin, it will exist in eternal limbo. According to Reformed theology, unelected babies will go into eternal hell because of their guilt for participating in Adam's transgression.

John Wesley wrote one of his few extended treatises on original sin and in it taught that no one will ever go into eternal hell for Adam's sin alone. Of original sin and its possible punishment in hell, Wesley said, "But *that any will be damned for this alone, I allow not,* till you show me where it is written. Bring me plain proof from Scripture, and I submit; but until then I utterly deny it."[25] Wesley preferred to believe that "unbelief is the damning sin."[26]

H. Orton Wiley and many others have taught in the same way. Wiley is surely correct in saying that the free gift of Romans 5 which came upon everyone to nullify our condemnation is a blanket removal of our guilt due to Adam's sin—but not of our depravity. Because of this racial benefit of Christ's atone-

---

23. W. B. Godbey, *The Incarnation of the Holy Ghost* (Louisville: Pentecostal Publishing Co., n.d.), p. 46.
24. George D. Watson, *A Holiness Manual* (Boston: Christian Witness Co., 1882), p. 51.
25. Wesley, *Works,* 10:223.
26. *Ibid.*

ment, if one is justified at the time of his death, he would go into eternal bliss—original sin being cleansed away for such a person who is walking in the light, even as it is in the case of infants and small children who die.

The careful holiness teacher will usually not teach holiness or hell. That incorrect teaching seems to imply that if a person dies in the justified state, but is not sanctified wholly, he will enter into eternal hell. It is quite another thing to say that if a justified person willfully refuses light on holiness, and deliberately refuses to seek entire sanctification when he knows God wants him to, he would lose his justification by disobedience to God—and would go into perdition if he were to die in that state.

It is justification, and not entire sanctification, that changes one's eternal destiny. For entering into heaven, entire sanctification is not a necessity in the way that justification is. If we are justified, and walking in the light, Christ's blood will cleanse us of original sin in an imputed way—as it does, as mentioned earlier, in the case of infants and children; and this is so also of lifelong imbeciles.[27] It would be more correct to say, therefore, that entire sanctification is a significant imperative, and not (without explanation) that it is a necessity.

L. *Why is it so important to understand holiness doctrine correctly?*

It is important for a number of reasons. It answers the "why" matters, and not simply the "how to" ones—and the "why" ones are more basic. They are like the fuel which an engine burns. Quality holiness doctrine is important the way quality fuel is important to an engine. The basic error of People's Temple was that it sought to foster religious experiences with an almost complete disregard for accepted Christian doctrines.

To understand holiness doctrine more or less correctly contributes to intelligent seeking of God's sanctifying grace. It is true that some believers will enter into the second blessing even

---

27. If a person were in accountable years, and had refused Christ, then became altogether mentally ill for the rest of his life, he would go before God unjustified.

if it is not taught to them in basically correct ways. Many believers, however, will miss out on receiving entire sanctification because it has been taught incorrectly at important points.

Also, and similarly, if holiness doctrine is taught correctly at its essential points, Wesleyan Christians, wherever they may be found, will be more effective in propagating it and leading others into the experience. Not only will such more-or-less correct teachings help us to propagate holiness doctrine in our time; it will help Wesleyans to bequeath the doctrine and experience to the next generation in its authentic and meaningful purity.

It is hoped that this chapter, and all the chapters in this book, will contribute, even in a small way, to these ends.

Scripture Index

Subject Index

Index of Persons
(Biblical characters not included)

A Bibliography
on the
Doctrine of Holiness

Arndt, William F. and Gingrich, Wilbur, eds. *A Greek-English Lexicon of the New Testament.* Chicago: University of Chicago Press, 1957.
Arthur, William. *The Tongue of Fire; or, The True Power of Christianity.* New York: The Methodist Book Concern, n.d.
Barker, John H. *This Is the Will of God.* London: Epworth Press, 1954.
Brengle, Samuel L. *The Guest of the Soul.* London: Marshall, Morgan and Scott, Ltd., 1936.
Brockett, Henry E. *Scriptural Freedom from Sin.* Kansas City: Nazarene Publishing House, 1941.
Brown, Charles E. *The Meaning of Sanctification.* Anderson, Ind.: Warner Press, 1945.
Bruner, Frederick Dale. *A Theology of the Holy Spirit.* Grand Rapids: Eerdmans, 1970.
Carradine, Beverly. *The Old Man.* Louisville, Ky.: Pentecostal Publishing Co., 1899.
————. *The Sanctified Life.* Louisville: Pentecostal Publishing Co., 1897.
————. *The Second Blessing in Symbol.* Louisville: Pickett Publishing Co., 1896.
Carter, Charles W. *The Person and Ministry of the Holy Spirit: A Wesleyan Perspective.* Grand Rapids: Baker Book House, 1974.
Carter, Charles W., and Earle, Ralph. *The Acts of the Apostles.* The Evangelical Commentary. Grand Rapids: Zondervan Publishing Co., 1959.
Cattell, Everett Lewis. *The Spirit of Holiness.* Kansas City: Beacon Hill Press of Kansas City, 1977.
Chapman, James B. *Holiness Triumphant.* Kansas City: Beacon Hill Press of Kansas City, 1946.
————. *The Terminology of Holiness.* Kansas City: Beacon Hill Press of Kansas City, 1947.
Church, John R. *The One Baptism That Jesus Offers.* Louisville, Ky.: The Herald Press, n.d.
Clark, Dougan. *The Theology of Holiness.* Chicago: The Christian Witness Co., 1893.
Clarke, Adam. *Christian Theology.* Systematically arranged by Samuel Dunn. New York: T. Mason and G. Lane, 1840.
————. *Clarke's Commentary.* 6 vols. Nashville: Abingdon Press, n.d.
————. *Commentary on the Holy Bible.* Abridged by Ralph Earle. Grand Rapids: Baker Book House, 1967.
————. *Entire Sanctification.* Louisville: Pentecostal Publishing Co., n.d.
Cook, Thomas. *New Testament Holiness.* London: The Epworth Press, 1941.
Cox, Leo G. *John Wesley's Concept of Perfection.* Kansas City: Beacon Hill Press of Kansas City, 1964.
Dayton, Donald W. *Discovering an Evangelical Heritage.* New York: Harper & Row, 1976.

Dunn, James D. G. *Baptism in the Holy Spirit.* Studies in Biblical Theology, Second Series. Naperville, Ill.: Allenson, 1970.

Earle, Ralph. "Acts." *Beacon Bible Commentary,* Vol. VI. Kansas City: Beacon Hill Press of Kansas City, 1965.

Ellyson, Edgar P. *Bible Holiness.* Kansas City: Nazarene Publishing House, 1938.

Fenelon, Francois de la Mothe. *Christian Perfection.* New York: Harper & Bros., 1947.

Finney, Charles G. *Charles G. Finney: An Autobiography.* London: Hodder & Stoughton, 1882.

———. *Lectures on Systematic Theology.* Oberlin: James M. Fitch, Co., 1847.

———. *Lectures to Professing Christians.* New York: Fleming H. Revell Co., 1878.

———. *Power from on High.* Fort Washington, Pa.: Christian Literature Crusade, 1944.

———. *Sanctification.* Edited by William E. Allen. London: Christian Literature Crusade, 1949.

Fletcher, John. *Checks to Antinomianism.* 2 vols. New York: Carleton & Porter, n.d. (There are several later reprints of this work from other publishers, including Beacon Hill Press, 1949.)

———. *The Works of the Reverend John Fletcher.* New York: Methodist Episcopal Conference Office, 1836.

Ford, Jack. *What the Holiness People Believe.* Birkenhead, Cheshire: Emmanuel Bible College and Missions, 1954.

Geiger, Kenneth (ed.). *Insights into Holiness.* Kansas City: Beacon Hill Press of Kansas City, 1962.

———. (ed.) *Further Insights into Holiness.* Kansas City: Beacon Hill Press of Kansas City, 1963.

———. *The Word and the Doctrine: Studies in Contemporary Wesleyan-Arminian Theology.* Kansas City: Beacon Hill Press of Kansas City, 1963.

Girvin, E. A. *Phineas F. Bresee: A Prince in Israel.* Kansas City: Pentecostal Church of the Nazarene Publishing House, 1916. Reprinted 1981 by Nazarene Publishing House.

Godbey, W. B. *Baptism of the Holy Ghost.* Greensboro, N.C.: Apostolic Messenger Office, n.d.

———. *Holiness or Hell.* Louisville: Pentecostal Publishing Co., 1899.

———. *Incarnation of the Holy Ghost.* Louisville: Pentecostal Publishing Co., n.d.

Gould, J. Glenn. *The Spirit's Ministry.* Kansas City: Beacon Hill Press, 1945.

Greathouse, William M. *The Fullness of the Spirit.* Kansas City: Nazarene Publishing House, 1958.

Hardy, C. E. *Pentecost.* Louisville: Pentecostal Publishing Co., 1927.

Haynes, B. F. *Fact, Faith and Fire.* Nashville: B. F. Haynes Publishing Co., 1900.

Henschen, Walter G. *Christian Perfection Before Wesley.* El Monte, Calif.: Deal Publications, n.d.

Hills, A. M. *The Cleansing Baptism.* Manchester: Star Hall Publishing Co., n.d.

———. *Fundamental Christian Theology.* 2 vols. (Cf. Vol. 2) Kansas City: Nazarene Publishing House, 1931.

———. *Life of Charles G. Finney.* Cincinnati: Revivalist Office, 1902.

Howard, Richard E. *Newness of Life: A Study in the Thought of Paul.* Kansas City: Beacon Hill Press of Kansas City, 1975.

Jessop, Harry E. *Foundations of Doctrine.* Kansas City: Nazarene Publishing House, 1938.

Jones, Charles E. *Perfectionist Persuasion: The Holiness Movement and Amer-*

ican Methodism, 1867-1936. Metuchen, N.J.: The Scarecrow Press, Inc., 1974.

Kierkegaard, Sören. *Purity of Heart Is to Will One Thing.* Trans. Douglas V. Steere. New York: Harper and Brothers, 1938.

Kittel, Gerhard. *Bible Key Words from Theologisches Worterbuch zum Nuen Testament.* Trans. J. R. Coates. New York: Harper and Brothers, 1951.

Knight, John A. *The Holiness Pilgrimage.* Kansas City: Beacon Hill Press of Kansas City, 1973.

Lindstrom, Harald. *Wesley and Sanctification.* London: The Epworth Press, 1946.

Martin, I. G. *Dr. P. F. Bresee and the Church He Founded.* Mansfield, Ill.: I. G. Martin, 1936.

MacDonald, William. *The Scriptural Way of Holiness.* Chicago: Christian Witness Co., 1907.

———. *Another Comforter.* Boston: McDonald, Gill & Co., 1890.

McLeister, Ira Ford. *History of the Wesleyan Methodist Church of America.* Syracuse, N.Y.: Wesleyan Methodist Publishing Assn., 1934.

Metz, Donald W. *Studies in Biblical Holiness.* Kansas City: Beacon Hill Press of Kansas City, 1971.

Morrison, G. H. *The Weaving of Glory.* Louisville: Pentecostal Publishing Co., 1900.

Mudge, James. *Growth in Holiness Toward Perfection, or Progressive Sanctification.* New York: Hunt and Eaton, 1895.

Nichols, James. *The Works of James Arminius,* 3 vols. Auburn & Buffalo: Derby, Miller and Orton, 1853.

Palmer, Phoebe. *The Promise of the Father.* Boston: Henry V. Degen, 1859.

———. *The Way of Holiness.* New York: Palmer & Hughes, 1867.

Payne, Thomas. *The Pentecostal Baptism: Is It Regeneration?* London: Christian Herald Office, n.d.

Peck, George. *Christian Perfection.* New York: Carlton & Phillips, 1855.

———. *The Scripture Doctrine of Christian Perfection.* New York: Lane & Scott, 1850.

Peck, Jess T. *The Central Idea of Christianity.* Louisville: Pentecostal Publishing Co., n.d. Abridged edition by Beacon Hill Press, 1951.

Peters, John Leland. *Christian Perfection and American Methodism.* New York: Abingdon Press, 1956.

Purkiser, W. T. *Conflicting Concepts of Holiness.* Kansas City: Beacon Hill Press, 1953.

———. *Sanctification and Its Synonymns.* Kansas City: Beacon Hill Press of Kansas City, 1961.

Purkiser, W. T.; Taylor, Richard S.; and Taylor, Willard H. *God, Man, and Salvation.* Kansas City: Beacon Hill Press of Kansas City, 1977.

Quebedeaux, Richard. *The New Charismatics: The Origins, Development and Significance of Neo-Pentecostalism.* Garden City, N.Y.: Doubleday and Co., 1976.

Ruth, C. W. *Entire Sanctification.* Kansas City: Beacon Hill Press, 1944.

———. *Entire Sanctification Explained.* Kansas City: Beacon Hill Press, n.d.

———. *The Second Crisis in Christian Experience.* Chicago: Christian Witness Co., 1913.

Smith, Hannah Whitall. *The Christian's Secret of a Happy Life.* Westwood, N.J.: Fleming H. Revell, n.d.

Smith, Timothy L. "Christian Perfectionism and American Methodism." *The Asbury Seminarian,* Vol. 31 (October, 1976) : 7-34.

———. *Revivalism and Social Reform in Mid-Nineteenth-Century America.* New York: Abingdon Press, 1957.

164 / Entire Sanctification: *The Distinctive Doctrine of Wesleyanism*
————. *Called unto Holiness.* Kansas City: Nazarene Publishing House, 1962.
Steele, Daniel. *Gospel of the Comforter.* Boston: Christian Witness Co., 1897.
————. *Half Hours with St. Paul.* Boston: Christian Witness Co., 1904.
————. *Love Enthroned.* Boston: Christian Witness Co. New York: Nelson & Phillips, 1877.
————. *Milestone Papers.* New York: Phillips & Hunt, 1878.
Stevenson, Herbert F., ed. *Keswick's Authentic Voice.* Grand Rapids: Zondervan, 1959.
Symon, Vinson. *The Holiness-Pentecostal Movement in the United States.* Grand Rapids: Eerdmans, 1971.
Taylor, Richard S. *Life in the Spirit.* Kansas City: Beacon Hill Press of Kansas City, 1966.
————. *Preaching Holiness Today.* Kansas City: Beacon Hill Press of Kansas City, 1968.
Taylor, Willard H. "The Baptism with the Holy Spirit: Promise of Grace or Judgment?" *Wesleyan Theological Journal* 12 (Spring, 1977) : 16-25
Turner, George Allen. *The Vision Which Transforms.* Kansas City: Beacon Hill Press of Kansas City, 1965.
————. *Christian Holiness.* Kansas City: Beacon Hill Press of Kansas City, 1977.
Walker, Edward F. *Sanctify Them,* revised by J. Kenneth Grider. Kansas City: Beacon Hill Press of Kansas City, 1968.
Watson, George D. *A Holiness Manual.* Boston: Christian Witness Co., 1882.
Wesley, John. *Explanatory Notes upon the New Testament.* London: Epworth Press, n.d.
————. *Explanatory Notes upon the Old Testament.* Reprint ed., Salem, Ohio: Schmul Publishers, 1975.
————. *The Journal of the Rev. John Wesley.* Ed. Nehemiah Curnock. London: The Epworth Press, 1938.
————. *A Plain Account of Christian Perfection.* Reprint ed., Kansas City: Beacon Hill Press of Kansas City, 1966.
————. *The Letters of the Rev. John Wesley.* Edited by John Telford. London: The Epworth Press, 1931. 8 vols.
————. *Wesley's Standard Sermons.* Edited by John Telford. London: The Epworth Press, 1921.
————. *The Works of the Rev. John Wesley.* 14 vols. Kansas City: Beacon Hill Press of Kansas City, n.d.
White, Stephen S. *Eradication Defined, Explained, Authenticated.* Kansas City: Beacon Hill Press, 1954. 95 pp.
————. *Five Cardinal Elements in the Doctrine of Entire Sanctification.* Kansas City: Beacon Hill Press, 1948.
Wiley, H. Orton. *Christian Theology.* 3 vols. Kansas City: Beacon Hill Press, 1941.
————. *Hebrews.* Kansas City: Beacon Hill Press of Kansas City, 1959.
————. *The Pentecostal Promise.* Kansas City: Beacon Hill Press, n.d.
Winchester, Olive M., and Price, Ross E. *Crisis Experiences in the Greek New Testament.* Kansas City: Beacon Hill Press, 1953.
Wood, John Allen. *Autobiography of Rev. J. A. Wood.* Chicago: The Christian Witness Co., 1904.
————. *Perfect Love.* Rev. Ed., South Pasadena, Calif.: John A. Wood, 1894.
————. *Purity and Maturity.* Boston: Christian Witness Co., 1899.
Wynkoop, Mildred Bangs. *A Theology of Love: The Dynamic of Wesleyanism.* Kansas City: Beacon Hill Press of Kansas City, 1972.

Ron Mehl
"God Works the Night Shift"